Christmas Future

OTHER BOOKS BY VALERIE IPSON

Ideal High, a young adult mystery

OTHER BOOKS IN THE
HOLIDAY ROMANCE COLLECTION

Eleanor and the Christmas Carol Fudge
by TAMARA PASSEY

A Christmas Carol for Candy
by PEGGY URRY

Christmas Future

VALERIE IPSON

RIVERSIDE PARK PRESS

Christmas Future
Copyright 2018 Valerie Ipson
All Rights Reserved

No portion of this work may be reproduced in print or electronically, other than brief excerpts for the purpose of reviews, without permission of the publisher.

This book is a work of fiction. All characters, names, places, incidents, and dialogue in this novel are products of the author's imagination or used fictitiously. Any resemblance to actual person, places, and events is purely coincidental.

Riverside Park Press
RiversideParkPress.com
riversideparkpress@msn.com

Cover design by McKenna Lee, Sage Fox Designs

ISBN 978-0-9864246-6-3

Printed in the United States of America
First Printing November 2018

for my parents—past

& my children—future

"What's today, my fine fellow?" said Scrooge.
"Today!" replied the boy. "Why, Christmas Day."
"It's Christmas Day!" said Scrooge to himself.
"I haven't missed it."

CHAPTER 1
Anchorage: 40°
Phoenix: 92°

Blame the Christmas tree. The artificial scotch pine filled Scarlett's view every morning when the elevator doors opened on the downtown Anchorage Department of Commerce, Community, and Economic Development. And every morning she scowled in its direction before following the cheery, ugly garland adorning the outer gray fabric walls of the cubicle city where she worked. The office redecorating was someone's idea of a joke because the calendar clearly indicated October. The nineteenth to be exact, which also meant the Christmas project that consumed half the summer and much of the fall was a full month past her internship end date.

Exiting the elevator, she avoided eye contact as she made her way to her desk. With her head down, she could ignore the too-frequently expressed greetings of Merry Christmas or Happy Holidays. Some of her coworkers took her job way too seriously. They weren't heading up the Get-Alaska-off-the-naughty-Christmas-spirit-list assignment. That would be her. The one with zero Christmas spirit.

She couldn't blame her chilly mood entirely on the tree. Or on the tinselly garland either. Not even on the Christmas carols that her cubicle mate had been humming under her breath for a solid month. Just all of it together served to remind her of the previous Christmas.

As usual, Fisher from Development hovered in the hallway. "Did you hear back from Santa at *the* North Pole?"

Scarlett bumped her phone up to her ear. *Sorry.* She mouthed the word and shrugged a shoulder toward the device before disappearing into the space she shared with Trina Murray.

"Marley is dead," Trina announced.

"Well, I guess it's only fitting." Scarlett set her phone down and pulled at her gloves before dropping them in an empty desk drawer one at a time.

Trina put her hands to her hips, her long, dark hair swaying as she spoke. "Your compassion is underwhelming." Then she pointed. "I loved that fish. If he shows up in your dreams, don't blame me."

Continuing her morning ritual, Scarlett unwound a baby blue wool scarf from around her neck and tossed it into the same drawer. "Call me Scrooge if you want, but you also loved Marley number one, Marley number two, in fact, Marleys three, four, five, and six." She scrunched her fingers through her honey-colored curls. "And maybe seven. Was this number seven or eight? I forget."

Trina shot her a look. "It was seven. I don't count the Marley that didn't even make it home from the pet store."

Scarlett unzipped her white sweater-lined coat slowly, reluctant to give up its warmth. "There are two things I have come to count on since my arrival in Anchorage, being cold and your fish dying. I think they're related."

The office manager, Daniel Yazzie, appeared at the opening of their cubicle, his round form closing off the entrance. "Nice jacket, Scarlett, but save something for winter."

"It was forty degrees this morning. Forty!" She waited for him to pass out of earshot before widening her eyes at Trina. "And that's the third thing I can count on. Being harassed by the natives."

"I heard that," Daniel called back. His face appeared over the short wall above her desk. Clearly not out of earshot.

"My coat's coming off now. Are you happy?" She slid out of it with only a slight shiver as she acclimated to the cool office temp.

"Whatever gets the job done, I'm happy." He turned his

attention to Trina. "Lose the tropical beach posters. We're promoting the 49th state, not the 50th." He graced them with a wide smile before finally continuing on to his corner office.

"Says the man who spent his thirty-fifth anniversary in Oahu." Trina rolled her eyes. "And I'm jealous."

Scarlett draped her coat over the back of her chair, turned on her computer, and listened for the inevitable sound of Trina's office chair whirling behind her. Her coworker liked to talk.

"You meant born-here-native, right? Not Native-native."

"Um, sure." Scarlett took her seat, angling it only slightly to continue the conversation.

"Really, it's fine. Daniel's cool. You see how he teases me about my Hawaii hobby?"

"You mean obsession. Where are your leis and that huge conch shell?"

"I'm toning things down." She waved a hand toward her wraparound desk as if it was no big deal.

"Keep telling yourself that you have a choice in the matter." Scarlett swiveled her chair from side to side, anxious to dive into her to-do list. "I don't know if Daniel realizes there's nothing I want more than for this job to be done so I can go home." She had been working at it since the start of July, and there was no way she would make it through an actual winter. He could call her *cheechako* all he wanted, she was fine being a newbie. She had learned all she needed to know about Alaska. It was cold.

"There you go, talking about going again. I can't believe you want to leave me and Marley number eight."

"Trina, my native-Arizona self is slowly freezing to death. And are you serious, there's already a number eight?"

"I texted Heath. I'm picking him up on my way home from work."

"Heath is an enabler."

"Heath loves me. He just doesn't know how much yet."

"Marley number eight is going to meet an untimely death. He just doesn't know how soon yet." Scarlett twisted the office chair to face her computer screen. She wiggled the mouse and clicked to check her inbox for any emails from her brother, Royce, but she soon stopped scrolling. The lying liar had been ignoring her phone calls too.

Only one major hiccup in her campaign to showcase Alaska's Christmas spirit had kept her past September. But more than halfway through October, she was as far away from Phoenix and her fiancé Alan as ever. If only she hadn't been so desperate for a fat paycheck and the possibility of a sizable bonus.

Listening to anything her brother said had been her first mistake. "Come showcase Alaska," he exclaimed. "It's the perfect place to get lost." His over-the-top enthusiasm should have put her on alert. The governor's office wanted an outsider, someone with PR skills, to see the state with fresh eyes. And then, surprise, he had neglected to mention the internship was showcasing Alaska's *Christmas spirit*. At least they gave her the use of a vehicle.

Scarlett gritted her teeth when Trina hummed "White Christmas" under her breath. Lately it was either that or "Let it Snow, Let it Snow . . ." *Please, no.* The girl she shared a cubicle with had made the past three months bearable, but the long-distance relationship with Alan was wearing thin. She needed to go home and either set a wedding date or break up. Sadly, it was practically a toss-up at that point.

Last December had overflowed with happily-ever-after: college graduation finally, a wedding proposal as expected, and the upcoming launch of an event-planning business with her roommate and fellow marketing major. She and Lexi Bloom had dreamed about Ambrose & Bloom Events since the end of freshman year at Arizona State, and for a moment Scarlett's future was merry and bright.

Merry and bright? Trina's carols were getting to her.

Her coworker jumped up mid-hummed-chorus. "I almost forgot." Pulling a red-striped bag from her cavernous purse, she drew a box of candy canes out and set it on the desk next to Scarlett's keyboard. "For you."

"What is this?"

"If Arizona doesn't have candy canes then *they* deserve to be on the naughty list with Alaska."

"I know what they are. I just don't know *why* they are." Scarlett narrowed her eyes at the gift. "Don't tell me the stores are already selling this stuff."

CHRISTMAS FUTURE

"You can get them year round in North Pole. With the official logo even. Didn't you say you like candy canes?"

"No. I do not discuss candy canes except within the vicinity of Christmas. It's not even Halloween yet."

"Well, you've been working on a Christmas project, and it's not Christmas, so . . ."

When her coworker sighed like someone weary of trying to cheer up the resident grump, Scarlett allowed herself to soften. A little. "It was nice of you, Trina. I hope you didn't drive to the North Pole just for this, though."

"Remember, it's North Pole, not *the* North Pole. It's the name of a town. You don't say *the* Phoenix, do you? Anyway, my cousin bought them. She lives near there, and she came down over the weekend."

Scarlett's phone buzzed with a text. "It must be Monday. Daniel's trying to call a meeting." The sarcasm flowed easily.

"I know he's 'not the boss of you,' but would it hurt to give him a report now and then?" Trina chided.

"He's my liaison with the governor's office, that's it. But I CC him on the emails every week," Scarlett replied. Another Trina-sigh followed. "Look, I've said from the beginning that I could do this by myself, and I did. Every sponsor is lined up, even several more than expected. And the entry forms for the giveaway that highlight them are almost ready to go to press."

"Not without North Pole on board."

A second text popped up with one word: *Mandatory*. She raised the phone so Trina could read it. "Be my buffer?"

"No way."

Scarlett pulled on Trina's arm, "Please? I'll hike Flattop Mountain with you this weekend."

"No, you won't. You ditch me every single Saturday because you'd rather work than hike. I mean you might actually breathe fresh air, observe an eagle fly in the wild, or gaze on the most gorgeous clear blue lake ever instead of your computer screen. Why do you think I had to beg my cousin to come down?"

Scarlett opened her mouth with a retort, but Trina stopped her. "Don't say it, I know. It's all about the bonus. It's all about beating what's-her-name."

"I'm going to ignore your last statement, but, yes, I came because the money was good. I don't deny it. But I won't bail this time, I promise. Maybe." Her friend was standing, and Scarlett drew her toward the doorway. "Grab the candy canes. It will look like I'm making progress with North Pole."

On their way to Daniel's office, her phone buzzed again. A text from her brother. He took a break from chopping wood to find civilization. *Minor change of plans. Staying another month? $$$* the text read.

Baiting her with dollar signs. She took the internship only because what's-her-name Lexi had cleaned out their business account to finance her honeymoon. Scarlett needed fast capital to get Ambrose Events running in time to be official when she began planning the Van Doren fiftieth anniversary party in January. By herself.

She reread the text. Royce was always so not helpful with his cryptic messages. He'd make some vague statement but no details because, really, he knew nothing. He no longer worked for the state. He'd gone off the grid, as they said in Alaska, to live off the land.

Before entering, Scarlett perused the room through the glass wall of Daniel's office. Fisher from Development, and Hannah and Jared from Community and Regional Affairs occupied seats in front of the heavy wooden desk.

None of them took her assignment seriously. Who cared if a radio station in Washington, D.C. randomly decided which states listened to the most Christmas music and then published a *nice* list of the top ten best, as well as a so-called *naughty* list of the ten worst. As if that was an accurate measure of Christmas spirit. Who besides Micki Blanding, the mayor of Charlestown, whose ex-husband worked in the federal capitol building. The same Micki whose personal friend was governor of the state. After a few rant-filled calls, the story went, Governor Hunt authorized a campaign to promote Alaska at Christmas time.

Micki wanted Charlestown at the center of it, of course, but it was just a nothing spot on the map compared to Anchorage— *the Gateway to Alaska*. The slogan greeted Scarlett at the Ted Stevens International Airport when she arrived, installing confidence that maybe the city would also be the perfect *gateway* to promoting the state's Christmas spirit. Or possibly hope sprang from the breezy temperature that beckoned as she met her taxi on the sidewalk. She had boarded in Phoenix at a nearly unbearable 106 degrees. She'd been so naive back then, truly a newbie. So unprepared to have Christmas in her face 24/7, and to have each day colder than the last.

She and Trina clustered in the doorway to wait for Daniel, who was unexpectedly absent, but Fisher started right in. "Hey, Ambrose. I thought of a good slogan for you." He was about the same age as Scarlett and Trina, and he took every opportunity to give them a hard time.

Scarlett pasted a weak smile on her face and flashed Trina a look of "See what I have to put up with?"

He gestured wildly indicating a grand headline. "Alaska's Christmas Spirit. It's better than New Jersey's. Get it? Because they're ranked number one on the naughty list."

"I get it." Alaska was number nine which wasn't as bad as it could be for a worst list. And she'd heard that one before. She pulled out her phone to make herself look busy.

"'Better than New Jersey' is not that much of a compliment. I mean, c'mon, it's New Jersey." Hannah offered her opinion.

"Watch it. My mom's from there," Fisher said.

Hannah prodded his shoulder with her palm. "Thanks for making my point."

"Yo mahm's from New Joy-sey." Jared attempted an accent before adding his own dig. "Really you gotta beat Ida-ho-ho-ho. Then you get a pile of dough-dough-dough." He threw in some awkward dance moves.

It went against Scarlett's better judgment to engage in the conversation, but Trina couldn't keep from chiming in. "Beating Idaho which is number ten on the naughty list is not enough. She has to get Alaska on the nice list."

"It's a top-ten worst list, so would you say Idaho is above us or below us?" Jared cocked his head as if he was taking the question seriously.

"Does it matter?" Scarlett replied a little too pointedly, despite her best efforts to ignore them.

"Chill out." Hannah's accompanying condescending giggle forced heat along Scarlett's collar.

"No. I know what I have to do, and I don't need everyone reminding me of it. Not the Christmas tree assaulting me when I get off the elevator or the holiday greetings or the—"

"Don't take it out on us. It's the governor who's making a big deal of it," Fisher said.

"You mean Charlestown's mayor is. And D.C. is at the top of the nice list. If that isn't rigged." Jared shook his head.

Hannah rotated in her chair to face Scarlett. "Christmas is my favorite holiday, okay? My mom even books Dickens carolers for events. I know I'm not the only one who thinks there's a better mood in the office because of the project. No thanks to your mood."

Scarlett clenched her fingers around her phone. So Hannah was responsible for the garland and the tree because she loved Christmas. Or maybe she delighted in being annoying.

"Candy canes anyone?" Trina waved the box, obviously in an effort to clear the tension.

"Everybody scooch together. Scarlett, take a seat." Daniel ambled past them and rounded his desk, then eyed her directly. "First off, let me get your thoughts." He seemed to ignore everyone else, not even noticing Trina, who had nothing to do with the project.

Scarlett snatched the box from her. "I have North Pole candy canes for everybody. I think I'm making progress there because last time I called they didn't hang up on me." She punched a hole in the cellophane wrapper and handed the box around before sitting down.

Fisher stood to accept the treat before moving to lean against a row of file cabinets. "Have my seat, Trina."

"Glenda and Bo are the nicest people in the world," Hannah said as she claimed a candy cane.

Scarlett wanted to steal it out of her hands but leaned forward in her seat instead, mentally blocking out the sting of the girl's earlier remark. "What are you saying?"

"Why don't you have them signed on as your biggest sponsor? They're North Pole. They're Christmas." Hannah furrowed her brows in obvious mock confusion.

"It's not because I haven't been trying." Scarlett turned back to Daniel. "Everything else is perfect, you know that. One more thing, then I can be done and go home, where it's right now a balmy ninety-two degrees." She wouldn't mention that she still hadn't finalized a slogan for the campaign.

"The nineties? That sounds like h—" Daniel didn't look up, just focused on his computer screen.

"It's heavenly compared to high thirties," Scarlett interrupted.

Royce's text message. Suddenly the thought of it sent a tiny bolt of adrenaline zipping through her. "Daniel, what do you mean? My thoughts about what?"

"I wasn't asking about North Pole," he replied, still absorbed by his computer.

"Hey, why didn't New Jersey do better on the list? They've got The Boss. 'You'd better watch out . . .'" Jared attempted a Bruce Springsteen imitation.

"I don't like that version at all." Hannah shuddered noticeably.

Jared defended Springsteen. "It's not as bad as 'Last Christmas.' He gave her his heart and she just gave it away."

"Be smart this year and give it to someone special," Fisher said. "Right, Trina?"

"Worst song ever," she replied from the seat he'd given up.

"Only because they play it a hundred times a day." Hannah wrinkled her nose. "Just like Springsteen's." She crossed her arms over her dark brown blazer. The color matched her shoes, her eyes, and her pixie cut.

Daniel finally looked up. "You all are too young to appreciate The Boss, now focus. We don't need to be wasting Scarlett's time."

"What exactly are we focusing on?" She sensed that she might be the only one who was lost.

"You haven't talked to anyone at the governor's office?"

"Daniel. You know my brother always sent me like half of one percent of no information. Plus he doesn't actually work there anymore, so anything he says is pretty sketchy."

"Governor Hunt wants a Victorian Village," Hannah said.

"To be more accurate, the mayor of Charlestown wants a Victorian Village," Jared added.

Great. Community Affairs already knew about this. Scarlett let go of a breath. "I don't see what that has to do with the Christmas spirit project," she said, afraid of the answer.

"Ohio has one." Fisher folded his arms across his chest as if he'd said something profound.

Development knew too? Then his three words dropped on her like a sudden avalanche. *Ohio has one. A state that's on the good list.*

Daniel glared at the room. "Thank you everyone for sharing, but yes, apparently Mayor Blanding was in Ohio visiting her sister last December, and the Victorian Village was the highlight of her trip, a really big event."

Scarlett slid to the edge of her seat. "It doesn't sound like an event, Daniel. You're talking theme park. I do PR, marketing. That's why I got the internship. And it's October. No one can build a park by Christmas."

"It's something new. The governor thinks it's the answer to getting on the nice list." Daniel clicked a few more keys on his computer. "Or maybe he's just being snowplowed by Charlestown."

"What happened to highlighting what Alaska already has to offer? I'm just waiting for North Pole because you said I can't do it without them. And, of course, I still need to narrow down what to name the whole thing." *So much for not bringing that up.*

Daniel turned his computer screen around, completely ignoring her question. "Here's the Dickens Victorian Village in Cambridge, Ohio. Check it out and get some ideas."

Scarlett approached his desk. "Can we speak privately?"

"Think scaled down. You have a few booths, some traditional candy and Old World pastries, serve coffee, hire some Dickens carolers. You're set."

She lowered her tone. "You and my brother and the governor and now Mayor Blanding seem to be forgetting that my internship is over. I've only stayed because of the North Pole issue."

"Did your brother mention anything about an additional bonus?"

Her weak spot. "He may have texted a few dollar signs," she replied, hoping only he would hear.

"Last Christmas . . ." Jared hummed.

CHRISTMAS FUTURE

The phrase echoed in her head as if she needed the reminder. She was already getting paid well for the internship, with a bonus if she could rock Alaska to the good list. And now talk of another bonus on top of that. It would be just what she needed to start her event-planning business back home. But as sole owner, without Lexi's or anyone else's help.

"The governor might be able to pull in some sponsors."

"But a Victorian Village? In Alaska?"

"It's Dickens. It's Christmas. If Ohio can do it, why not Alaska? Neither one of us are London."

Another month. She could already hear Alan's protests. More than that, she imagined the cold and the ice and the snow that November was sure to bring. Scarlett's sigh reached the end of her toes. Toes vulnerable to frostbite if they stayed in this state much longer.

But the money. "Will I be home by Thanksgiving?" No sense completely freezing to death or ruining plans for the holidays.

"Not a problem."

Scarlett pointed at his screen. "It's not going to be that."

"But knowing you, I'm sure it will be amazing."

"I don't have time for amazing. The governor knows that, right?"

"The real question is does Micki Blanding know that? Charlestown has wanted a Victorian Village for years." Fisher gave voice to what Scarlett feared. She preferred working as a team of one, but a pushy mayor might challenge that. Obviously the mayor's desire to highlight the state's Christmas spirit was only a step to getting what she really wanted.

Daniel held out a neon green sticky note with a name and address listed on it. "There's a Dickens expert at the Wasilla Community College. I spoke to a secretary there who said you can probably pick up some reference material as early as Friday. So go. See if he can give you some direction and lend some authenticity to the whole thing."

"Dr. P!" Trina who had been quiet ever since Daniel came in, suddenly gushed. "I took a Dickens class from him. He's the nicest man, Scarlett. He'll be glad to help."

CHAPTER 2
Anchorage: 55°
Los Angeles: 83°

Gil stared at the nameplate that still adorned his late father's university office. *Gilbert T. Pennington, English Department.* He exhaled slowly. "Am I ready for this?"

The secretary, Darlene, jiggled the key in the lock with one hand and patted his arm with the other. The gesture reminded him of his sweet mother who had been gone two and a half years. "No one ever is, are they? I helped my sister clean out her husband's office a few months ago, and it was eye-opening to say the least. But you'll be fine. Your father was a good man." After unlocking the door, she held the key out to him. "Why don't you hang on to this, so you can come and go while you're working?" She touched his arm again. "Just don't tell anyone I'm giving it to you."

Gil slid the key into his pocket. "Thank you. And thanks again for being patient. My dad's funeral and burial were all I could handle last spring. A trip to Anchorage was not in the plan."

"It took some talking, but your father was well-loved. And really, no one will need it until January."

Gil held her gaze, not anxious to see what was waiting for him behind the door. "Darlene, was my dad happy here? I mean being in Alaska and teaching at the college?"

"Kind of a loaded question. I feel as if he was definitely

comfortable, but I could see in his eyes how much he missed his wife . . . your mom. She must have been a special lady."

"After she passed away, I wasn't surprised when he announced he was going to teach up here. Southern California had suddenly lost its appeal."

"It can go either way, really. Some want an immediate change, but for me, when my Stan died, I wanted to stay right there in the house we built together. That's where all the memories were, and I couldn't let them go."

"Of course, you already live here in God's White Earth. That's what my dad used to call it. He was from Fairbanks. California was a foreign country to him."

"He may have mentioned that a time or two." Darlene smiled. "But when he talked about your mom, I could tell it was home."

Gil stared at the nameplate again.

Darlene stepped back, apparently to give him some room. "Sometimes the first step is the hardest. Should I open the door for you?"

He laughed. "I'm sorry. You probably have work to do. And you've already done so much. I don't know what job description says you have to arrange for a person's body to be shipped out of state to be buried next to their spouse."

"In a snowstorm, no less." Darlene shook her head. "No, I get it. I want to be buried next to Stan, no matter what." She patted his arm one last time. "I'll let you get to it then. The empty boxes you asked for are right here, and I'm at the end of the hall if you need anything else." She left him to his task.

On the plane from Los Angeles he'd considered this moment of opening the door and what he might find inside. In his emails back and forth with Darlene, she had said that his dad seemed to spend more and more time in his office, sometimes sleeping on the narrow futon instead of going home to his townhouse, and often barely taking time to eat. It was no wonder his health had declined so quickly before a heart attack took his life.

Or maybe Gil worried more about seeing his dad's Alaska, a place that existed only in stories around the dinner table and in Gil's imagination. Not that he anticipated bears and moose around every corner. More likely he feared a loss of the magic that emanated from the telling and retelling.

He reached for the doorknob, twisted, and gently shoved the door open. A pungent mustiness assaulted his senses just as his cell phone rang.

"Sorry to bug you. It's Darlene. Two things I forgot to mention. First, I had all the items from the storage unit brought over. Since you wanted the furniture sold, there really wasn't much left, mostly some clothes and kitchen things. Books that he couldn't fit here, I think. Anyway, they're sitting in the back office for when you're ready. No rush."

He'd definitely forgotten about the stuff from the townhouse. Maybe she had forgotten she promised to air the place out.

"Gil, are you there?" Darlene's voice sounded through the phone.

"Yes. Thank you for taking care of that." He breathed slowly to acclimate to the smell.

"Did you get the door open?"

"Just barely."

"Take it slow. You can do it."

"I don't have a choice. I didn't spend all day on a plane for nothing." His restless night in the hotel hadn't helped his mood either.

He ended the call with Darlene, but just as quickly his phone rang again. "Hey, Gil. You didn't answer last night. I guess you made it all right?"

"I crashed as soon as I got to the hotel." His sister didn't need to know he'd had trouble sleeping.

Izzy had taken the lead in cleaning out their parents' house when Dad decided to move after Mom's death, so it was only fair that Gil tackle the office. Besides, she'd just given birth to her second baby, and staying put was a necessity. He knew packing up an office couldn't compare to doing the same with a house full of twenty-five years of living, even with hired packers and movers in the mix. Plus his dad was going from a respectable, though solidly middle class, twenty-four hundred square feet to a one-bedroom, one-bath setup. What to keep, what to give or throw away—that had been the hard part.

CHRISTMAS FUTURE

Gil had driven out to see the empty house, to walk through with Dad and Izzy one last time before saying goodbye at the airport. Dad was right, it wasn't home without Mom.

"Is it as cold as they say?" was Izzy's next question.

"Colder." He quipped. "Fifty-five for the high today. It actually feels good. Do you remember when dad used to tell us randomly what the temperature was in Alaska?"

"He'd compare it to whatever it was in Los Angeles like we were all wimps or something." They shared a laugh.

"Now I'm going to be hearing his voice every day I'm here, 'Do you know what the temperature in Alaska is today? It's eighteen degrees.'" *Fond memories.* "How's Ember?"

"She actually slept for three hours straight last night. It's progress."

"And how's Penn taking it?"

"He's demanding equal time on my lap, so there's that. I'm sure he's much nicer to his sister than you were to me when I was born, though."

"Hey."

"I remember the stories Mom used to tell."

"Tell him Uncle Gil is coming to visit and can give him all the lap time he wants. I'll settle things here and come for Christmas. Maybe Thanksgiving if I don't get a better offer."

"Ha, ha. Penn will love it no matter when you come." She paused. "How was it leaving your kids?"

Gil leaned against the open door, facing the hall where the air was not so dank. "Harder than I thought. I had no idea when I promised to practice at Riverside County clinics that I would get so close to people. I just looked at the scholarship as a way to get through school without student loans."

"And I'm so jealous. I hate student loans."

"You should have seen the families, Iz. They had going-away parties at every clinic, and they brought piles of gifts, like the most amazing homemade quilts and salsa. I tried to tell them I was getting on a plane for Alaska and I couldn't take anything, but they didn't care."

"I know from the stories you've told how much they love you."

"I didn't want my three years to end. Is that crazy?"

"Because you are a nice person, Gil. You care about people, not money."

"Except I'm going from the underserved of inland California to the rich-y rich of LA."

"I know. What's that about?" Izzy teased.

"I guess it's a done deal. I start in January."

"Not until then?"

"I just want a break to take care of Dad's stuff and find his Dickens manuscript. That publisher from London keeps calling."

"So how's Dad's office?"

"I haven't made it past the doorway, but it's a mess, if that makes you feel any better."

"Wish I were there to help."

"No you don't. Anyway, it's my turn."

"Hey, I bet more than one publisher would be interested in the manuscript. Sometimes they go to auction and get crazy amounts of money."

"I'm not worried about the money, Izzy."

"Yeah. 'Cause you don't have student loans, you jerk," she teased again. "Look. I know Dad put his heart into every one of his books, but it's not like the manuscript is something personal that we need to hang on to. It's a file on a computer. There's no sentimental value. Just sell it to the highest bidder."

"I know. You're right."

"Now when you find the hand-carved nativity, I want that. He very specifically made sure to take that with him."

"I'll keep you posted."

"I'd better go see what Penn's up to. Love you, Gil."

He slipped the phone into his back pocket. Since Mom and Dad were gone, Izzy was the only immediate family he had. Of course, his brother-in-law, Shawn, and his nephew and new niece were part of the family, and that made it all the better.

If he concentrated on finding the nativity, maybe he could hurdle the mental barrier of going through his dad's things. He picked up the smallest of the boxes and ventured inside. He'd start with the source of that smell first.

The office was a decent twelve by twelve feet, but the desk, the futon, and the bookshelves lining every available wall space combined to create an even more closed-in feel. Papers littered some surfaces, even the floor, but the trash can sat empty. Some rumpled dress shirts and a few pairs of slacks lay over the far end of the futon, but upon inspection he determined they smelled clean. He yanked on the latch of the small, narrow window on the back wall and shoved it open. The room just needed a good airing out.

Dad spent his final days here. Gil shook away the thought. Maybe he should have insisted his father stay in LA instead of moving so far away from family. Of course, Izzy was already far away in Spokane, Washington, and Gil himself had been a busy physician with long rotating hours at the clinics. Still he'd try to get to town at least every other weekend once Dad finished promoting his last book. Dad had written three, all based on the life and novels of Charles Dickens. Gil perused the bookshelves quickly, expecting to see them displayed prominently together.

He dropped the box and began stacking papers. The books would turn up eventually. Hopefully the nativity would too. His dad had carved it after Mom saw a similar one while in England on a trip paid for by royalties, and Gil wanted nothing more than to surprise his sister with it. Dad's last Christmas gift to Mom would become a family heirloom passed down to her children. Izzy must have mellowed with maternity. She hadn't even given him a hard time about when he was going to add to the family.

A knock on the open door interrupted his thoughts. "Come on in, if you dare," he called.

A woman bundled in cool blue and white took one tentative step into the room. Her blonde curls framed a pretty face that was barely visible between the snow cap and scarf. "Dr. Pennington? I'm Scarlett Ambrose from . . ."

He watched her eyes as they took in the room from one end to the other.

"Is this a bad time? The secretary was on the phone so I just kept on walking, but . . ." She put a hand over her mouth. She must have gotten a good whiff.

"Gil?" Darlene's voice drifted in from the hall before her face appeared behind the girl in the doorway, forcing the blonde to slide farther inside. "Oh, now that's fragrant!" The secretary peeked her head in. "I am so sorry. I meant to let some fresh air in the place before you arrived. Keep that window open whenever you're here and give it a day or two. Should be fine."

He laughed because her look said otherwise. "Either that or I'll acclimate. And no need to apologize, you've done enough."

She waved away his comment. "You're being too kind. Anyway, that other thing I forgot to tell you—a man named Daniel called about someone stopping by. I'm guessing it's you, Miss . . . ?" She gestured toward the stranger.

"Ambrose. Scarlett. I'm so sorry for just showing up without an appointment." She grimaced toward Gil. "I was told the end of the week might be good, and I couldn't wait any longer."

"Is this about Dickens? Someone called me too."

"Daniel's my boss. Well, not really. He's more like a liaison."

"I told him I wasn't even close to being ready." Gil fought the resentment rising in his throat. He'd been clear on the phone. "It's going to take some time to go through everything. And even then, I'm not sure what my plans are."

Darlene backed away. "I'll let you two sort this out," she said before leaving.

"I'm sorry. I guess I misunderstood. I didn't mean to interrupt…this." Scarlett shrugged. "But I need some information to take back to my office. Anything to kind of get things moving in the right direction, you know."

Gil swept the rest of the papers from the desk into a box. He'd sort them later. "I can't help you right now. I've got a lot going on, not just the office, but personally. Give me a month or two. Call me then." Even though he agreed with submitting the manuscript to a publisher, he wasn't ready to hand it over to the first person who asked.

"Uh, no, I'm sorry. I don't have a month or two. Christmas is coming, and my job is counting on this."

Gil dragged a couple of neckties from the closest shelf. "He kept it?"

"Excuse me?"

He looked up. "It's nothing. Just a rock I painted for my dad when I was at Scout camp. I think I was twelve. I can't believe he actually kept it." Gil held it up toward her, then realized how awkward it must have looked getting excited over a silly rock from probably sixteen years ago. He rubbed off a layer of dust before setting it back on the shelf. "'Bah! Humbug!' It was one of our dumb jokes."

"Dickens, right?"

"Of course."

"Just curious. Why the focus on Dickens, I mean, that author specifically?"

"When your dad's an English professor and your mom's obsessed with *A Christmas Carol*, it just happens naturally."

He knelt down near the bottom shelf to tug on a plastic bin with a tight lid. *If Dad kept the rock then the nativity is here somewhere.* He worked the corner up to reveal yellow legal pads scribbled with his dad's handwriting.

"Well, that's why I'm here. Because I need an expert."

She was going to press the issue. He slid the bin back in place. "Let me stop you again. If I haven't been clear, then I'm sorry too, but I can't do this now. Maybe wait until I call you?" He hated to be so firm about it, but he had told them on the phone. It wasn't his fault they sent out this really nice girl to plead their case. He had barely arrived in town. He flat-out was not ready.

He felt a twinge of regret as she slipped out and closed the door quietly then reminded himself of the mess he had to deal with. Actually, reminding wasn't necessary. He was standing in the middle of it.

CHAPTER 3
Anchorage: 42°
Phoenix: 92°

    The foyer Christmas tree accosted her as always Monday morning, and so did Trina when Scarlett arrived at their cubicle.
    "Tell me how it went with Dr. Pennington. Didn't I tell you he's just the nicest man?"
    Scarlett removed her hat and gloves before answering, Trina's question serving as a chilly reminder of her visit to the college. "Dr. Pennington is not only not the nicest man I've ever met, he practically threw me out of his office."
    "No way. Not Dr. P. Did you say something negative about Dickens? I warned you to be nice."
    "He didn't even want to talk about it, Trina. He said call him in two or three months, then he said, 'No I'll call you.' That was practically our entire conversation."
    Trina was clearly confused. "You had the wrong office or something. There's no way," she repeated.
    "Professor Gilbert T. Pennington. I read the nameplate next to the door. It was his office, believe me." Scarlett removed her gloves and hat. "The whole place was a mess, and he was in the middle of organizing it, I guess, but that doesn't mean he had to be rude. And how long does it take to clean an office anyway? He could spare me a few minutes."
    Trina plopped into her desk chair. "I still can't believe it. Professor. Gilbert. Taylor. Pennington?"

"How many professors with that name do you think there might be at a small college like Wasilla Community?" Scarlett unwound her blue scarf.

"Did you say, 'My friend took your class'?"

Scarlett pressed everything into the desk drawer, while she waited for her words to sink in.

"Did you say, 'Trina Murray read *Great Expectations* when she was a freshman because of you, and she loved it'?"

Scarlett pulled off her coat and draped it over the back of her chair.

"Did you say, 'You're my only hope for a decent Dickens Village that will rival Ohio's'?"

"Trina, are you listening to me? Your name did not come up. The words Victorian Village did not come out of my mouth." She eased into the thick cardigan she kept in her office for cold days. Every day. "It was a complete waste of time. I drove all the way up there for nothing. A big fat zero."

"I should have gone with you."

"He wasn't in the mood to talk. In fact, he hardly talked at all except to say, 'Let me stop you' and 'How about I call you.'"

"No way. Not Dr. P."

"All I've got so far is Dickens carolers lined up, but I'm back to Googling Victorian Villages, so can we talk about something else?" *Or not talk at all.*

"Have you seen the new intern? He was in Daniel's office wearing an olive green T-shirt better than anyone's ever worn a T-shirt. And his hair is the color of—"

Scarlett held up a hand to stop her. "I get the picture. I hope Daniel remembers that I work alone." She woke up her computer. "Unless, by chance, he's an expert on Victorian Villages."

"I wouldn't get anything done with him around, if you know what I mean."

"How's Heath doing?"

"He's great, thanks. And since we're mentioning the men in our lives to keep from thinking about the guy in the T-shirt, how's Alan?"

"You're the only one thinking about the intern. I've been reliving my unpleasant encounter with the rude professor, and

Alan is being, well, Alan." She brought up her daily calendar.

"Is that a good thing?"

"Just the usual. 'When are you coming home? When are we setting a wedding date?' Can you believe he actually wants me to bail on this project? He doesn't get that I made an agreement to see this through. Even with the new Victorian twist."

Their coworker Fisher poked his head into their cubicle. "Scarlett, Daniel wants you in his office. ASAP." He paused a moment as if he wanted to say more, either to her or Trina.

"Fisher?"

"Sorry, that was it." He continued down the hall.

"He didn't actually use the word mandatory like last week."

"Scarlett. Just go."

"He's going to ask how Dr. Pennington can help us, and I've got a big fat nothing."

"You mean zero. You said big fat zero," Trina kidded.

Scarlett made a face. "Thanks for clarifying."

"Do you want me to come?"

"Will you?"

"Are you kidding? I did that last week, and you didn't go hiking with me."

"You didn't even go." Scarlett knocked over Trina's plastic Hawaiian hula dancer on her way out of their office space.

"Keep your frozen cold fingers off my hula girl!" Trina called.

Scarlett hung a right past the last row of cubicles and then slowed a bit as she took in all the bodies inside the glass walls of the office manager's office: Daniel, Fisher, Hannah, Jared, and an unknown brunette in a royal blue, form-fitting, sleeveless dress. Scarlett shivered and wrapped her sweater more tightly around her front. And there was a guy waiting outside the door in an olive green T-shirt. She stopped. *Dr. Pennington? He's here?*

She wanted to turn around. Claim she got tangled up in the persistent Christmas garland that lined every single surface. He had better be there to apologize, to beg forgiveness for having such poor manners. He'd better have come crawling back with a stack of resources on Dickens Victorian Villages.

Daniel looked up at just the wrong moment to wave her in.

CHRISTMAS FUTURE

"Scarlett, come on. Everyone scooch together. There's room." There really wasn't, but she planted herself inside the open door as far as she dared, completely ignoring *Dr. P* on her way in. She did not feel inclined to *scooch*, no matter how much Daniel liked that word.

"This is Scarlett Ambrose, our transplant from Arizona. She's in charge of the Christmas spirit project. Scarlett, I just wanted to introduce you to Carole London from LA. KWIX hired her to do segments on their midmorning show. They're calling it 'Christmas Carole.' With an *e*. How much do you love that?" He beamed at the room. "She'll be doing Christmas crafts and baking, but with an Alaskan flair. You'll go on the show a few times to promote the state's vacation giveaway and the Victorian Village."

Except Scarlett would be gone by Thanksgiving.

The group parted a bit to allow her and Carole to shake hands. She didn't get a rugged Alaskan feel from this girl. Or a homey, crafty, "Christmas tree-shaped cookies in the oven" feel either. That's obviously not what KWIX graded on.

"Welcome to Alaska. I trust you've found it to be as cold as I have." Immediately she realized how that sounded. "I meant the weather, not any of you . . . you know, really warm people," she lied. If there had been space, she would have gestured to prove her inclusiveness. "Nice, friendly, warm people," she repeated for emphasis, but her fellow employees weren't about to let it slide.

"Nice try, Scarlett," someone from the far side of the mosh said. Sounded like Fisher.

"It takes cold to know cold," came from Hannah.

Daniel held up a hand. "Zip it, people."

Scarlett disregarded the insults. She knew how they felt.

"I'm sure Daniel said it already, but we're happy to help in any way." At least she knew how to politely offer support. Unlike a certain professor, who, fortunately for him, chose to stay glued to the outside wall with no possibility for evil-eye contact.

"And Scarlett, this is Hudson Lewis, the producer at KWIX. He's your guy for all the publicity spots." Another handshake. This one attached to a slick, seasoned professional dressed in upscale, classic business attire and a wide, practiced smile.

"All right, let's get back to work. Hudson and Carole, thanks for coming by, and welcome to the team." Daniel began a sweeping double wave that meant the meeting was over.

No explanation as to why Dr. Pennington was there, or any mention of the apology he owed her and, really, all of Alaska. Or at least the governor. And there was no team, she wanted to say. She was it.

Daniel's voice stopped her. "Hey, Scarlett. Can you stay a minute?"

She wasn't going to get out of a report. Maybe Dr. Pennington should stay too. Actually come into the office and explain why he wouldn't share his Dickens expertise for the good of the state's Christmas spirit.

She shimmied toward the wall of file cabinets to let the other luckier souls pass into the hall. Did Christmas Carole really just cozy up to the professor as she exited? But then there was no mistaking what she said, "Meet you at the elevators, Gil. I have to talk to Hudson for a minute." Then she squeezed his arm before falling into close step with the TV producer. Not that Scarlett was paying attention.

"Can you close the door?" Daniel gestured toward it.

She obeyed and then turned back, bracing herself for his questions.

"Maybe you should sit."

She obeyed him again. Did she sense awkwardness all of a sudden? Why was he being so formal?

"First, I have some good news. Mayor Sprouse, of North Pole fame, faxed her agreement. They'll be part of the campaign."

Hallelujah! This was not the kind of news to sit for. She wanted to do cartwheels down the cubicle corridors. Instead, she opted for sinking deep into her seat as relief flooded to her core. *Finally!* It didn't mean she could go home because the Victorian Village still loomed, but . . . *finally!*

"Now name the campaign and send it to the printer."

"I'm working on it, Daniel, but I want to get it right."

"Scarlett, you're talented. I know why they gave you the internship. But . . ." He appeared to be weighing his words.

CHRISTMAS FUTURE

Wait. Was this the sitting-down part?

She was struggling, but she wanted to complete the assignment. She had agonized all week about her choice to stay longer, had even gone over the pros and cons with her mom and then Alan, over the phone. It came down to reality. And reality came in the form of a monthly bill for rent on what was supposed to be the home of Ambrose & Bloom Events, a hole-in-the wall space that sat empty in Scottsdale, Arizona. She hadn't been able to cancel the contract.

"I know why they put you on this Christmas spirit project, but the thing is . . . you don't have any . . . Christmas Spirit."

Any possible retort dropped from her throat to her stomach like a lump of coal.

"I know it sounds crazy, but the department is trying to have fun with this, and they feel you're bringing down the mood."

Surely by department he meant Hannah. "This is because I complain about the tree and the garland? Did you know there are actual campaigns to ban Christmas music prior to December? And people protest store shelves being stocked with holiday items before Halloween."

"I'm only talking office morale and the cooperation you need from everyone. This project is something different. It's actually making things a bit more, should I say . . ." He paused.

"What, Daniel?"

"Merry?"

She wasn't sure whether to take offense or consider herself above all this nonsense. "So you're saying I'm killing the 'merry'? Never been told that before." Scarlett let out a long breath.

"Do you even like Christmas?"

"Who doesn't like Christmas, Daniel?" It came out more pointed than intended.

"I had to ask."

"Just because my best friend cleaned out our business account on Christmas Eve so she and her brand new husband could pay for a honeymoon they couldn't afford, why would I not like Christmas?" She leaned forward in her chair. "Maybe I'm a little more 'bah humbug' than 'ho, ho, ho' right now, but for the good of the 'merry,' I'll keep it to myself." She stood up, in no mood to talk about her failed trip to the college.

Daniel appeared blindsided. "I'm sorry about what happened with your friend, but will you take some advice?"

Scarlett braced herself against his desk.

"Quit holding Alaska at arm's length. It's an amazing place, and no matter what that radio station in D.C. says, we have a lot of spirit. At Christmas and every time of year."

Daniel let her go without further comment, but she rounded the corner straight into the person she most wanted to avoid. She decided not to hold back.

"Dr. Pennington. I came late to the meet-and-greet, so what'd I miss? Now suddenly you're on board with helping us?" Looking better in a T-shirt. Forget the T-shirt, the creamy, milk chocolate eyes, trimmed hair the color of . . . Somehow, she'd missed them at their first meeting. "I'm surprised you unburied yourself from that mess in your office."

"Scarlett, right? So you're not from the publisher in London."

"I'm pretty sure Daniel explained to the secretary on the phone that I was coming from the Department of Commerce, Community, and Economic Development." She kept her look impersonal.

"That's a mouthful." He scrubbed a hand through his khaki brown hair giving it sort of a windblown look without the wind. "I was wondering why you didn't have an accent. I had to assume you were one of their American agents."

"I'm confused. What does this have to do with the Christmas project?"

"Exactly. You came to my dad's office for a completely different reason. Not at all related to publishing his Dickens manuscript."

"Your dad's office?"

"Yeah. My dad's." His brows conveyed his confusion. "He passed away last spring, but I wasn't able to come clear out his things until now."

"So you're not Dr. Pennington. Figures. You could have told me." She raised her shoulders. "Why didn't you tell me?"

"I am Dr. Pennington, so I didn't realize the need to correct you. Why didn't you tell me who you were?"

"I told you my name. I don't generally pose as someone else."

"I meant tell me where you were from, that you were with a project from . . . whatever the name of your department is."

"Would you have been more polite?"

The confusion on his face lingered again. "Look. Long story. And the work facing me in that office wasn't helping."

"No more explanation necessary, Dr. Pennington. Not the real Dr. Pennington, but it doesn't even matter. I've got work to do, and I believe Christmas Carole wants to meet you at the elevators." She immediately regretted letting the last phrase slip. She didn't need him thinking she was concerned at all about his personal business.

"Cari . . . Carole . . . I'm just here with her. But let me apologize for how you think I acted." He smiled and even seemed to be suppressing a laugh.

"How I think you acted? Wow." His audacity floored her.

"If it matters at all, I'm a primary care doctor." That smile again. "I just finished a three-year contract practicing in Southern California. Now I'm done and have some time to settle my dad's affairs. Uh, I mean clean out his office and decide what to do with his research and collected papers. Plus he has a manuscript I need to do something with."

"You're a doctor. Great." She covered her face with her hand. After a pause, she said, "It seems I'm the one who owes you an apology."

"Have you ever had to go through your parents' things after their deaths? It's not easy."

"I'm sorry. I'm sure it wouldn't be." Her eyes strayed to the T-shirt. At least he was smart enough to wear long sleeves. And that shade of green really was his color. On second glance, pretty much any color qualified for that distinction. "I should . . . you should . . ." She pointed in the direction of her cubicle.

Before she could finish another coherent sentence, Carole appeared from the direction of the lobby. "Well, thank you for keeping my fiancé company. I thought he got lost."

"I, yeah." Scarlett pulled her phone from her back pocket. "I missed a call from my Alan, I mean my Arizona." She pointed at her phone as if it might magically turn her lie to a truth. "My fiancé Alan in Arizona. Nice to meet you both." She tapped the screen and lifted it to her ear to continue the pretense, but the doctor kept her gaze.

"Wait. Maybe I can help. If I find any reference books about Dickens or Victorian Villages would you still be interested?"

He seemed sincere, but she hesitated.

Carole molded her body to her fiancé's side. "I've seen his dad's office. Stop by later tonight and I'm sure we'll have a bunch of crap to dump on you."

Did Dr. Pennington just wince when Carole called his dad's stuff crap? "I am desperate, so I guess . . . yeah. I can probably drive up," she conceded.

They turned toward the elevators while she sidestepped her way into her office space to Trina's immediate exclamation of "Scarlett!"

It was then she realized her phone was still planted at the side of her head. She placed it on the desk and put a finger to her lips. "Are they gone?" she whispered.

Trina craned her neck to look over the cubicle wall in an exaggerated fashion. "I. Think. So."

Scarlett released a long breath and dropped into her seat.

"Who was that? What was that? You talked to him for ten minutes," Trina demanded.

"I'll tell you one thing. He is not the new intern."

"Spill. Spill."

"That's Dr. Pennington. Junior." She emphasized the last word.

"That's the Dr. Pennington you met with? No way."

"Oh, no, yeah. Apparently Dr. Pennington Sr. died last spring." She stopped when Trina's jaw slacked open. "Oh, sorry to blurt it out like that. Are you okay?" Her friend waved her on. "That was his son. The one who practically threw me out of his office. Turns out he thought I was a publisher after his father's Dickens manuscript or something."

"He came to apologize?"

"Not really, no."

"I'm telling you, Scarlett. That guy is gravy."

"Gravy?"

CHRISTMAS FUTURE

"You know, from *A Christmas Carol*. When I was in the play in high school, me and the other orphan girls used to call the really hot guys gravy and the people we didn't like 'an undigested bit of beef' or 'a fragment of an underdone potato.'"

"What?"

"Have you never read *A Christmas Carol*?" Trina deserved a prize for her dramatic gasping. She took Scarlett's silence as the pathetic no it was. "And you're in charge of a Dickens Village. For shame, you 'blot of mustard,' you 'crumb of cheese.'"

"Now you're making me hungry for an early lunch. And, well, Gravy's engaged to Christmas Carole."

"Whoa. Explain."

"Did you hear about the TV segment KWIX is doing? I just met the hostess with the mostest, and her name is Carole, and the show is, you guessed it, Christmas Carole."

"Really?"

"With an *e*. She's part of the team now." With air quotes for team. "It's a tie-in to the Victorian Village, and they want me to go on the show, except I'll be in Arizona by then, so I could care less about any of it."

"Is he really a doctor? Because I suddenly feel like I'm in the market for a new one." She only wanted to talk about the doctor.

"I think you're in the market for something."

"Don't tell me you were not even a little bit attracted."

"He's engaged. I'm engaged. End of story. Plus I just made a huge fool of myself, so thank goodness I'm taken. He's taken. We're all taken."

"I'm not."

"What about Heath?"

"Grr. Marley's dead."

CHAPTER 4
Anchorage: 42°
Los Angeles: 84°

"What were you discussing with that girl? Scarlett, is that her name? It must have been funny. At least you thought so."

After waiting several hours back at the TV station for Cari to meet the crew and be oriented about the show, Gil had trouble focusing on their conversation on the drive to the restaurant for a late lunch. Fortunately she did most of the talking, but his thoughts kept straying to the girl needing advice about Victorian Villages. It startled him that Cari was thinking of her too.

He scrambled to come up with a reply before pulling to the curb. "It's a long story. And not funny." He'd only wanted to lighten things up, but maybe he really had been rude to her when she appeared at his dad's office.

He handed his keys to the valet before opening the door of the rental car to let Cari out. He gave his name to the girl waiting at the entrance with menus, and then they followed as the hostess led the way to a table by the window.

"How is anything here a long story? You arrived last Friday," Cari said.

"Thursday," Gil corrected. He reached for her hand and rubbed at the spot where her engagement ring should have been.

She pulled away. "I told you I can't wear my ring at the TV station. It's better if they think you're unattached. Oh, look at that view, Gil. The lake is gorgeous. Wouldn't it be even prettier at night." She nuzzled his shoulder, then took the seat he offered.

30

CHRISTMAS FUTURE

"From now on stay away when I'm on the set or around anyone involved in production. You almost gave me away today at the tourism office." She slapped his hand with her menu.

"I don't think it's a tourism office, but so what if they know you're Cari Smith. TV people have stage names."

"I really want to play the part. Is that so wrong? I want Anchorage to see me as Christmas Carole, all about Christmas. It will look great on my resumé."

He wanted to say that no one cared if someone named Carole went by Cari, but it wasn't worth the effort. They were supposed to be enjoying their first break in a long time, with neither of them working.

A server in standard white shirt and black dress pants approached the table. "My name is Marcus, and I'll be serving you this afternoon. What can I get you started with?"

Gil looked at Cari. "Champagne?"

"Ah, we're celebrating today." Marcus nodded. "I like the sound of that."

Cari flashed him a smile. "I'm going to be appearing on Midday Anchorage starting in late November. Just signed the contract this morning."

"Congratulations. I'll have to check it out."

Once they received their entrees, Cari was back to her question about Scarlett. It was no big deal. He wished she would let it drop. He just wanted to dig into the King salmon that Alaska was known for.

Her phone lit up with her ringtone. "I have to take this call. Yes, this is Tiffany." Her voice glided up an octave. "Top three? Really? Thank you for letting me know . . .Yes. Yes, I'll look forward to hearing from you . . . Definitely. When I'm back in town I'll give you a call. No, should be soon. End of the week maybe. Lunch would be perfect." She singsonged her goodbye, then set the phone down.

"Tiffany?" Gil's eyes widened. "What was that?"

"I'm top three for the jewelry show. And believe me there were a ton of gorgeous girls auditioning."

She hadn't told him about a jewelry show.

"They're hiring a couple of new hosts for the season, and if they like you it could become permanent, but, of course, these things always lead to other bigger and better things." She relaxed back in her chair. "Top three!"

"What happened to Christmas Carole, all about Christmas?"

"A jewelry show in LA trumps anything in Alaska."

"You signed a contract this morning." He tried to keep his tone light, but it was a battle.

"My agent can get me out of it if I need to." She sipped her champagne. "This is how you play, Gil. You keep your options open. You keep the plates spinning until they all fall but one. It's not like being a doctor. It's okay for you to have one plate, one option."

"I have options."

"Not anymore. You paid your debt to the reservation, now you're free to become the 'most compassionate primary care physician in the Greater Los Angeles area.' That's what that online article said about you. And we can start planning the wedding." She dug into her salad.

He could already sense a to-do list forming in her head, but his indignation was rising, egged on by the fact that she continued to call Riverside County the reservation. He let out a long breath. "Just wondering, will I be marrying Cari Smith, Carole London, or Tiffany . . . sorry I didn't catch her last name?"

"Shut up and tell me about the girl at the office."

Scarlett, who said she never posed as someone else. They ate in silence for a few minutes.

"It was a misunderstanding," he began in between bites. "She came by my dad's office. I thought she was a rep from the publisher. She thought I knew that she was working on a Dickens Village."

"And you found that funny?" Cari speared a cherry tomato.

"Not really. She thinks I was rude."

"She's probably right. You're so touchy about your dad's manuscript. Just sell the rights. I've been trying to tell you."

"Can we enjoy eating and not talk about it?"

"I'd enjoy lunch way more if I knew that you were getting that huge advance. Who says no to that much money, Gil? Don't you think your dad would have been thrilled that his work was worthy of a number that high? Of course he would be."

CHRISTMAS FUTURE

"I wish I knew what he wanted." Gil wasn't only uncertain about the manuscript. He was feeling uneasy about his decision to practice in LA. Inheritance money from his dad allowed him the luxury of time to decompress after the rigors of the previous three years and medical school before that. He hoped spending a little down time in Alaska would help crystallize his goals.

"Forget about the Dickens stuff for now, we're celebrating your new gig," he said. "And we'd better hurry before it becomes your old gig. Here's to Christmas Carole." He raised his glass to hers just as Marcus placed their check on the table.

Cari set down her champagne and grabbed her phone and purse. "Enough celebrating. We should get to your dad's office."

"I thought we'd take the night off since you just got into town."

"Gil, you're here to clear out your dad's stuff. That's all. One more glass of champagne, and then I'm out of these heels and digging into that mess."

Later they let themselves into Professor Pennington's office. "There's something so sexy about this."

Cari wrapped her arms around his neck and kissed him, but his thoughts were on their lunch conversation. He did have options.

She drew his face to hers to force eye contact. "Somewhere in this office is something someone will pay big money for. It's like buried treasure."

He pulled back. "Buried on the computer anyway. But I really want to find the nativity my dad carved for my mom."

"You're worrying about Christmas decorations?" She leaned in to kiss him again. "Somewhere here is the key to our future," she whispered in his ear.

The door opened, and Darlene stuck her head in. "Oops, sorry to interrupt. I'm on my way out, but I was just informed that someone's proposing at the bell with video and everything. I don't know how long you expect to be here, but they're asking if people can be gone by eight or go out the back way. I'll warn you, though, that will mean a long trek to the parking lot."

Gil looked at his watch. "We'll be gone by then."

"Was that the bell tower we passed on our way in?" Cari asked Darlene. "I could tell something was happening."

"Yes, it's in the quad. In fact, you should be able to see it from here." Darlene left them alone again.

Cari immediately peeled herself from his side and stepped around boxes and stacks of books to the narrow window. "They're putting up white lights. They've got a sound system. Bags of rose petals? Gil, you won't believe this. Heaters! They brought in those tall heat lamps. Who is both this thoughtful and romantic?"

Gil ignored her. That question had already been beaten to death over the past year. Instead he dug into the closest bookshelf on a search for anything related to Victorian Villages or nineteenth century London. If Scarlett showed up, he wanted to have something to give her.

"Did you hear what I said? It's not you, that's for sure."

"You're right." He didn't have the energy to argue.

"You could surprise me with a real proposal."

A real proposal. He waited for her words to fall with a dull thud between them before replying. "Didn't you really say yes?"

Cari tore herself away from the window to return to his side. She kissed him again. "I'm kidding. Let me enjoy this."

When did kidding feel so exhausting?

"Knock, knock." The voice along with a snow hat and puffy white coat announced Scarlett's arrival. "Um, sorry," she said.

Gil pulled back from Cari to arm's length. "Come in if you can find a path. I just started a stack for you." He could see her surveying the room as she had when she dropped by Friday. "You don't notice any progress—is that it?"

"Some of the piles appear more organized, I think." She seemed to suppress a smile as she removed her hat and gloves. "I got the third degree coming in: Where am I going? How long am I going to be here? I have to leave out the back doors."

"It's a proposal. Come look." Cari returned to the window. "It's so romantic."

Scarlett appeared unsure but then joined her after navigating the office maze.

"Those bags are full of rose petals," Cari declared, as if any self-respecting marriage proposal had an abundance of rose petals.

"They're rolling out a red carpet," came from Scarlett, and

they both sighed audibly.

"Now you're just ganging up on me." No response. To them he wasn't even there. He chose a box to load with the Dickens reference books and went back to the shelf he'd been working on, determined to ignore their oohing and ahing. Women and wedding proposals. Maybe he failed at both.

"But those heat lamps. If I was getting engaged in Alaska, heat lamps would seal the deal," Scarlett said, and both of them giggled.

Gil concentrated on books as their chatter continued in the background. After gathering several he carried the box to the desk.

Cari turned suddenly from the window, her phone in her hand. "You know what, Gil? I gotta run. Hudson wants to meet for a drink and go over some set ideas. But, hey, you've got some help right here." She clutched the other woman's arm in a dramatic fashion. "Please, help him get this organized. We will pay you." She rolled her gaze to Gil.

He hesitated, not sure what to say. Scarlett was simply there to pick up reference books.

When he didn't reply, Cari continued, "I will pay you." She navigated her way to the door. "Love you, babe. Call me as soon as you find something."

"Bye." He let the word fall since Cari was already out the door. She hadn't filled a single box.

CHAPTER 5
Anchorage: 32°
Phoenix: 67°

    Scarlett stared out the office window at what must have been the hopeful groom, possibly his mother, and a scattered group of siblings and/or friends setting up for the proposal. The event planner in her was loving it, and not facing Gil made her embarrassment easier to hide. She was alone with him again with nothing to talk about except for the reference material he filled a box with so intently. They'd already covered the fact that he'd been rude to her at their first meeting, yet here she was again because he had been nice enough to offer help once he knew what she really needed.
    She attempted to concentrate more on the scene out the window and less on him. "I wonder what their story is," she ventured, hoping to cover the silence that Carole had left behind. "They must have met here at the college. Monday is an odd day for a proposal. It must mean something." She halfway hoped he'd ignore her. That she could just take the books and go.
    She hadn't planned on the white sky shedding its soft edges—delicate flakes that blinked in the muted glow of the lit courtyard. She hadn't expected the way her jaw would drop with wonder at her very first Alaskan snowfall. "It's starting to snow," she pronounced in a breathy whisper.
    "Snow?" Gil's footsteps behind her told her he wanted to see for himself.
    "Now it's perfect," she added.

"Perfect's going to last for about ten minutes. Then it's going to be a wet, slushy mess. Just one more newly minted fiancée with issues about her marriage proposal."

His comment drew her out of her reverie. "You speak from experience, Doctor?" There was definitely a backstory.

"You know you don't have to call me doctor. Gil is fine."

Was he deflecting? "Gil hardly seems enough when your name is Gilbert Taylor Pennington II." She hadn't moved from her spot even though he had come in close.

"How did you know?"

"People call you Gil, so I made an assumption." She hitched her shoulder. "I hope Carole didn't leave because of me." She turned away to put some space between them.

After one look out the window, he backed away too. "When TV Producer Guy calls, what're you going to do?"

"That's nice that she got a job in Anchorage while you're here. I can't imagine Alan ever coming. All I'm hearing from him is 'When are you coming home?'"

"Alan?"

"My fiancé in Arizona. That's where I'm from." She twisted the diamond on her finger. The action seemed to catch his attention, so she stopped.

After a pause he said, "Can you blame him?"

"He should know me. I'm a planner. I sign contracts. I fulfill them. Like I'm just going to bail on Alaska's Christmas spirit?"

Gil actually laughed out loud. "I guess when you put it that way. But generally people want to be with the person they're engaged to."

Scarlett bit her bottom lip, and allowed her gaze to wander to the door, still open from Carole's exit. Maybe it was rude to look. Maybe he didn't notice.

"Like you said, sometimes work keeps you apart."

He'd noticed. "She has a contract," she offered in Carole's defense, hoping it might cover the awkwardness.

He raised his eyebrows, but if he was going to say something he was interrupted by a beefy fist banging on the office door.

"New furniture's here." The beefy guy attached to the fist

stopped and stared at the boxes, books, and papers that filled the space. "Dudes, did you literally not get the memo?" He rotated his head out of view. "Hey, Rocky, this guy didn't get the memo." Laughter filtered from down the hall.

Gil met him at the door. "What furniture are you talking about?"

"Old desks out. New desks in. Shoulda been ready to go."

Gil pulled out his phone. "Let me make a quick call. Sorry about this," he directed the apology at Scarlett. "I'll call Darlene and then carry the books to your car."

She tiptoed to the futon, unsure of how to make herself useful. She would sit until he was ready.

"Hey, it's Gil," he said into the phone. Suddenly his eyes widened in her direction, then froze into an unsettling look of alarm. His conversation with Darlene became punctuated with one-arm gestures, and then he forcibly grasped her hand to lift her up. "Some guys say they're here with new desks. Do you know anything about that?" His actions didn't match his words.

His eyes held hers, and the look served to keep her in place, so she stood there, unsure of what he expected. At last he thought to let go of her, though it took several moments.

Soon he tapped his phone off and walked out to the hall without explanation. Over his shoulder, she could see Beefy Guy and Rocky lugging a desk out of the office across from them.

"Check your order," Gil said. "You're supposed to skip 107."

The one named Rocky set down his end of the desk and pulled out a slim electronic tablet from behind his back. She didn't want to think about where he'd stashed it since it was way too big for his back pocket. "Gilbert T. Pennington, number 107. What do you know, Tyler? We're supposed to skip it." Tyler grunted a reply as they hauled their load down toward the exit.

Gil pointed to the window and the desk in turn. "Snow's falling, desk is staying. Oh, the proposal outside is frightful, I mean, perfect. Now what was it you came for?" He flashed a grin. "Kidding. Dickens reference books coming right up. And despite what Carole, said, you do not have to help me with cleanup."

He picked up the box of books and made it as far as the hall before looking back to see she had stayed rooted in place.

"Are we going to ignore the fact that sitting on the futon is an apparent capital offense?" she asked.

"The futon." Gil let out a slow breath before sliding the box onto an empty shelf. "Darlene just learned from one of the janitors this morning that my dad was found on the futon. After his heart attack."

His words didn't need any length of time to sink in. "Ohhh," she exhaled. "I'm so sorry. And a bit freaked out." She covered her mouth with her hand. "And sorry I just said that."

"I know what to do." He was back in the hall looking both ways, then arranging with Tyler and Rocky to take the futon with them for disposal. One hefted the frame across his shoulders, and the other followed with the cushion. For a fee.

Soon they were back for payment. "Do you know what's going on out in the quad tonight?" asked Tyler.

"The proposal! What time is it?" Scarlett clambered to the window. A light dusting of snow had fallen on an idyllic romantic scene. Everything was in place, even the videographer who was hiding in the bushes, though all she could identify was a hunter green wool cap and a heavy coat holding a camera. "You guys can't be taking furniture out. A marriage proposal is about to happen."

"What? We got an order here." Rocky reached around to his backside for the tablet.

"No, please. I don't want to see that electronic device ever again." She held up her hands in protest. "I know you have an order, but it has to wait."

"Huh?" This came from both guys.

"Videographers cost a lot of money. I'm an event planner. I know these things. I haven't started my business yet, but I've been doing it for years for family and friends. You don't want to become immortalized for eternity on someone's proposal video."

"Whoa, what are you talking about, lady?"

"We're just clearing out furniture." They spoke over each other.

"But we're almost in lockdown. No one leaves the building unless you go out the back way." *Why are they so dense?*

"Not gonna happen. Our truck is right outside those doors."

"This is seriously the moment they'll be telling their kids and grandkids about on every anniversary. Gil, tell them."

"Hey!" a voice yelled from down by the exit. "Someone move this truck, ASAP!"

Scarlett gave the movers her best "I told you so" glare. "It looks like you've got most of the desks out into the hall. Just come back and load them after 9:30." She shrugged and gestured to emphasize her point, then softened her tone. "Okay. Go home, tell your wives or girlfriends the story. They'll say what a romantic you are for holding off on loading the truck so someone can get engaged. They'll bring hot chocolate, snuggle with you by the fire, give you a nice backrub."

The guys burst out laughing. Even Gil couldn't keep a straight face. "You've been reading too many Hallmarks," Tyler said.

Scarlett gritted her teeth in an effort to stifle her reply. This was not her event. She was not responsible for making sure the engagement went off without a hitch. *Deep breath.* But these guys were jerks, and the doctor wasn't helping.

She checked her watch and reached for the box. "I guess I'd better take my books and leave before I'm stuck going out the back way myself." She hadn't meant it to sound so abrupt, but books were what she had come for. Just books. Why was she still there?

Gil reached for the box too. "I got it," he said. She detected a note of apology in his voice. "Guys, you heard her. Get lost. If you don't want to come back until tomorrow, I can tell the secretary what happened."

"I guess we'll at least finish pulling desks and go," one said to the other.

"Whatever," came the reply.

Instead of leading the way into the hall, Gil turned with the box and laid it on the desk.

When he didn't immediately speak, she chimed in, "We have to go. Well, I mean, you do what you want, but I have to." She gestured toward the door. As if on cue she heard Tyler and Rocky banging desks next door and laughing about hot chocolate and back rubs.

"I'm sorry about those guys," Gil began.

CHRISTMAS FUTURE

She interrupted. "Please don't apologize for them."

A cream colored book with a festive wreath and dark green lettering on the spine caught her eye. She pulled it from the shelf. *Dickens at Christmas.* "You were holding this one back?" Then she noticed the author name. "Your dad wrote this? Oh, I'm sorry. You probably don't want to lend it."

"No, I'm glad you found it. I haven't made it around to that shelf yet." He took the book from her when she held it out to him. "Isn't it terrible, I haven't even read it? Med school," he offered as an excuse.

Tyler and Rocky passed by with a desk and a few more choice words about having to come back to load.

Gil tucked the book under his arm and reached for the door. "Mind if I shut this for a minute."

"Please do." There was still almost fifteen minutes before proposal time. Enough time to get out of the building.

He handed the book back to her. "Take it, but I was thinking. Can I get your number in case I come across anything else?"

"Sure, okay." She scribbled her number on a notepad he found in the desk. "You must have had the best Christmases growing up. I mean, anyone whose dad writes things like *Dickens at Christmas*." She ran her hand over the glossy cover before cracking it open to the dedication page. *To my Marie, who always knew how to keep Christmas well.* "Aww. I'm guessing Marie is your mom."

"Yes. Let me see."

She flipped the book around and held it out for him to read. "What does it mean?"

"It's one of the last lines from *A Christmas Carol*. My dad might have written the books, but it was Mom who knew how to keep Christmas."

His tender answer touched her. "Now I'm even more curious."

"She believed that at Christmas time you needed a little noise and a little quiet. Noise was all the fun of Santa and presents and going north to go skiing with cousins. Quiet was dimming the lights and singing songs around the tree and Dad reading the story of Christ's birth in Luke from the New

Testament. We had to have both to make the holiday complete."

"That is beautiful, Gil. So you mentioned something before about a manuscript. Your dad wrote another book?"

"I can't even tell you the title of it, but a publisher wants it, and everyone seems to think I should just submit it and accept the advance."

"And you're hesitating because . . . ?"

"It's my dad's work. I want to do right by him." The scraping and bumping increased in the hall and then against Professor Pennington's office door specifically. Then more laughter, some of it muffled probably by a beefy fist.

"I'm glad they're enjoying themselves, I guess," Scarlett said.

"Something's off." Gil marched to the door and pulled it open. The entire way was blocked with desks piled one on top of the other. "What the . . . ?" Gil heaved his shoulder into the heap, but it budged only a bit.

Scarlett joined him to add her weight to the heave, but it didn't help. "I can't believe they would do this." The desks were heavy-duty wood and metal, and stacked on top of each other they were a formidable barrier.

Gil leaned into them again. "Seems like they've got more desks behind these." He slid his fingers around one end attempting to yank it to the left. Then he tried the other end. From the banging and grunting, they knew the two guys were still close, adding desks to the right of the doorway.

"Why do I suddenly feel as if I'm in the middle of a senior prank?" Scarlett raised her voice, hoping it would carry. She placed her face in the slight gap between desk and door jam. "And in high school, not college."

Gil joined her at the gap to add his frustration. "This isn't funny, guys. Move the desks!"

One of them called out, "No time. Someone's about to get engaged."

Irritation seethed through her. "I take back what I said. You'd better go home and give your wives foot rubs and tell them what total jerks you are to make up for being such jerks. But I bet you don't even have wives. Or girlfriends."

"We're on lockdown, lady!" Then they heard a door slam.

CHAPTER 6
Anchorage: 32°
Los Angeles: 61°

Neither Gil nor Scarlett spoke for a few moments. He looked at her, but she only stared at her watch.

"It's 8:00 straight up," she said.

He ran his fingers through his hair. "Guess who's getting a front-row seat at an engagement. At least a window seat anyway."

Her mouth drew into a thin line. She obviously wasn't finding humor in his comment.

"This is my fault," she stated. She wandered over to the empty space where the futon had been and then seemed to realize that fact, so headed over to the window. "I think work is getting to me. It was a rough day. I was going to pick up these books, grab a bowl of Tomato Basil from Ruby's, to go, and soak in the bathtub at the hottest temp I could stand." She looked around the small office. "And then work a couple of hours. So much for that plan."

He grabbed a metal standard-issue office chair from a corner, then changed his mind and rolled the softer, cushioned one from behind the desk. "This is all I have to offer, but I'll work on that obstruction."

She sat. "I like your professor-son's big words, but it's not going to budge."

"But if I don't at least try, what sort of show of manliness is that?" He flashed a grin. "Then after I fail, I'll call Darlene.

She's the only one I have a phone number for at the college, but she'll know who to contact."

"What about Carole? TV Producer Guy looked pretty buff. If I'm remembering correctly, of course." Her smile flashed back.

"Now you've left me no choice." He plastered himself against the desk mountain and pushed. After a few feigned grunts and moans he stopped. "How was that?"

"Call Darlene," she deadpanned.

The call went straight to voicemail, so he sent a text as well. "I guess I'll try campus security or the Wasilla Police."

"You really don't want that Hudson guy coming to your rescue, do you?" Scarlett threw in another dig.

"I will not be asking him to drive up from Anchorage, if that's what you mean." Gil found a number for the police station, and after an interminable amount of rings a woman's voice came on the line. He struggled to explain their situation while keeping a straight face. Not an easy feat since Scarlett seemed amused by his attempts.

"How's that proposal going?" Gil said when he was put on hold. Scarlett stepped to the window, but not before he caught the laughter in her eyes. They were an interesting shade of gray. Maybe green.

"So far they're no-shows," she said before relaxing back onto the chair.

"Maybe dinner went long?"

"Or they had a fight." Scarlett swayed in her seat.

"The fight isn't at dinner. That comes after the engagement, when the girl starts picking apart the proposal and finds it lacking."

"I knew it. There is a backstory. Let's hear it."

"I don't believe in beating dead horses." He turned to the window. "Shouldn't there be some kind of support team for this? I was thinking we could yell out the window and get someone's attention." Finally the woman came back on the line to explain someone would be on the way soon.

"They're sending someone," he reported.

Scarlett stood up next to him. "Anyone helping is half-frozen by now and cursing the groom-to-be for choosing an outdoor venue. I'm sure they're inside somewhere."

"You know your event planning stuff, don't you?"

"When I'm done with this internship, I'm going back to Phoenix and opening Ambrose & Bloom Ev— I mean Ambrose Events."

"Bloom bailed?"

"Bloom cleaned out our business account to pay for her honeymoon. The honeymoon that I told her was way over budget. Like why do people want to start their married life together in debt? I'm all for whatever kind of event, party, or celebration you want, if you can afford it. And the irony is, she didn't put that trip on her credit card after all, she just robbed our savings. Sorry. Don't get me started." She sat back down.

"I think I already did." He felt the glare she gave him, so he tried to cover. "And that explains why you're thousands of miles away, somewhere extremely cold, doing a job you don't like."

"I needed the money, but I had to get away too." Her answer was straightforward without emotion.

"Did she ever pay it back?"

"I closed the account and blocked her phone number." Scarlett left her seat and began to pace. "There's an envelope right now on my parents' kitchen counter that Lexi left for me, and it's probably my part of the money. Our savings was mostly hers, but we had a dream and a plan. Once we got going, I would make up the difference." Scarlett stopped to look at him, as if gauging his reaction. "My mom keeps asking if she can mail it to me, but I can't deal with it."

"So it's less about the money and more about her reneging on your deal." He meant it more as a statement than a question.

"Exactly, but now I have to be about the money, or she'll never see that I can do it without her. That's why I have to get Alaska on the good list by coming up with a Victorian Village, of all things."

She explained her internship, how she majored in marketing and, at the time, her brother worked in the governor's office and recommended her. How she wasn't really a Scrooge, but it had been Christmas Eve when she discovered the empty bank account. Her coworkers called her assignment "Christmas in July," but now it was October, and the decorated office was driving her crazy. And if all that wasn't enough, she was going to freeze to death before it was over.

Gil did his best to listen and nod, realizing she needed to vent. He couldn't blame her. She was stuck in a twelve by twelve office with a near stranger after working all day and driving almost an hour to get here. It was dark out and snowing. And totally his fault his questions had caused her to tense up.

He owed it to her to move those desks, but after pushing and prodding, sliding and trying not to swear in front of her, he gave up again. "Check the window. Anyone out there yet?"

No one was, and it appeared they were stuck in his dad's former office due to an engagement that might never happen. At least until their help came, but no sign of that yet.

Scarlett wrapped her arms across her body. "Did the heat just shut off?"

"It'll come back on. Something about not letting the pipes freeze or they'll burst."

"So get me to a pipe because if I freeze, I might burst, and then what a mess you'd have . . . on top of this mess. Helping you clean out your dad's office is the worst proposal I've ever accepted." She narrowed her eyebrows, but he knew she was kidding. "And the heater has nothing to do with pipes. You're supposed to let a trickle of water run so pipes don't burst. Of course, in Alaska I have no idea if that's a thing. Doesn't everything freeze here? I know I do."

"Is that why you wear your coat even when you're inside?"

"I haven't been warm since July, so it's best just to keep it close."

They continued watching out the window. "Do you want to know what happened today? I actually got good news about a sponsor, one of my last loose ends for that particular project." She paused, then frowned before continuing. "But today Daniel told me I have no Christmas spirit."

He left her side without a word and returned with the painted rock. "I bequeath this to you, Miss Scarlett." He held out his palm where the smooth, oblong rock rested.

"The humbug rock? No, that's a treasure. You have to keep it."

"You don't understand. This is a magic rock." He ran his

fingers over the words in red. "'Bah! Humbug!' is the opposite of Christmas spirit, so the rock takes all the bad or angry thoughts, the stress and worry, all the negative stuff—it takes it away."

"Did your dad tell you that?"

"Yep. It became a running joke. We'd secretly leave it where the other person would find it. And sometimes when my mom or my sister were having a bad day, we'd conspire to leave it for them to find. Like in my mom's purse or next to my sister's toothbrush."

"That's so tender."

"They didn't always think it was funny, especially Izzy. She took it as a sign that we thought she was being a grouch, but we'd say, we only want you to be happy. Then we'd laugh because she was right."

"That's a sweet memory of your dad."

Gil passed the stone back and forth between his palms, the weight and smoothness of it spurring his thoughts. He held it out to her again. "So would you like to borrow it?"

"How about you keep it, but if I get really desperate I'll let you know."

The more they talked, the more she intrigued him. He was drawn to her gray-green eyes that brightened with her smile and alternately flared with righteous indignation. The way her twisty waves of hair, a color lighter than his own, spilled over the collar and shoulders of her coat that she didn't remove, even indoors.

Gil took up a post at the window again. "Hey, the cameraman's risking the cold. See, he just ran into the bushes over there. Do you think he'll hear me?" He reached for the latch, but at first yank it wouldn't budge. "Wow, now I'm oh for two in the manly department."

Scarlett nudged him out of the way. "I'm sure it's frozen shut. Just tell yourself that."

"Thanks a lot." He nudged her back.

"You can't yell out there now anyway. The couple must be here."

"It's about time. We don't have all night," he joked. "I don't want to pass judgment on the Wasilla Police force, but where are they?"

"By the way, it's a videographer, not a cameraman."

Gil studied her. "So do you have a video of yours?"

"My?"

"Proposal. When Alan from Arizona asked you to marry him."

"That. Actually I do."

"Keep going." He knew there was more to it. This would prove his point about women — never happy with their engagement stories.

"Let's just say he went above and beyond in the proposal department."

"I'm happy for you." His tone flattened, but Scarlett was quiet. "Aha! Don't hold back now," he urged.

Scarlett left the window to walk around the small perimeter of the room. "He orchestrated this whole humongous event. He was asking my roommate and my mom and my sister, and even texting my brother, who knows nothing, about what all my favorite things were. It was so bad that my roommate was asking me what my favorite love song was so it could be playing in the background. Basically I was planning my own proposal."

"But you're an event planner. You mean you didn't love being in on all the behind-the-scenes stuff?"

"Not at all. What about romance? Surprise? Something from the heart? Didn't he know I needed that?"

"He knew you're a planner. He was giving you exactly what you wanted."

"You're taking Alan's side?"

"Alan sounds like a great guy. Intuitive enough to think about what kind of proposal would make you happy. That's more than I can say for my botched attempt."

Suddenly Scarlett stopped mid-pace and waved a hand toward the door. "Look, I'm a hostage here. I'm missing Ruby's Tomato Basil and a hot bath. I don't care about dead horses, what went wrong with your proposal?"

The mention of the Tomato Basil again finally penetrated his thinking. "You must be starving."

"Actually . . ." Her voice trailed off. "But aren't you?" she finished.

"I had a late lunch. A big late lunch. Here." He wielded a

CHRISTMAS FUTURE

box of granola bars from the desk as if it would solve everything. At least he hoped it would help somehow.

"No offense, but what's the expiration date on those?" She grimaced slightly.

He couldn't keep from laughing. "I bought these over the weekend for when I was stuck in the office working."

"Stuck. Literally. But you're not getting any work done, and I've wasted your whole night. Carole was even going to pay me." Laughter shone in her eyes. "And you're not off the hook with your proposal story. Let me check the proceedings one more time, and then you may begin." She moved to look out into the quad, then checked her watch. "Still nothing. I'm worried about those two."

She made a show of getting settled onto the chair again and then looked up at him with exaggerated expectation. "Story snacks, please. I'll take two."

"One might be enough." He leaned against the edge of the desk and handed over the whole box, amused by her sense of humor. "I'm debating whether to call the police again."

"It's snowing. Maybe they're dealing with accidents."

"Maybe some Arizona drivers are out tonight."

"Ha, ha. As if you've ever driven in snow, Mr. Los Angeles. Now quit stalling."

"Here are the gory details. Last Christmas, Cari came to visit when I was working in Riverside County. We made the rounds at the little county hospital. I introduced her to my favorite patients, which is all of them, and the kids just loved her, and she loved them. She brought them dolls and stuffed animals and candy, and I guess I got caught up in the Christmas spirit, and after we walked out of the building we sat on a bench and I proposed. End of story."

Scarlett shook a granola bar at him. "Not end of story."

"Okay, it was the desert. We were in a little town on the border of California and Arizona. There were dust devils swirling and tumbleweeds rolling by, to hear her tell it."

"Did she say yes anyway?"

"She almost didn't. The first thing she said was, 'This couldn't wait until we get back to LA?'"

Scarlett was kind enough not to comment, but he knew what

her facial expression meant. *Who says that when they get proposed to?* "And I said, 'But where else are you going to find cactus but here?'"

"I'm guessing she didn't appreciate the joke?"

"You would be correct."

She bit into her granola bar and chewed for a few moments, but she wasn't done. He could read it in her eyes. "Did you put any thought into that at all?" she asked finally.

"I was overcome by the moment. Isn't that what you were just saying? Something not orchestrated, something from the heart?"

"But desert? Tumbleweeds? I don't know. And carried away by Christmas spirit? Really?"

"So a guy can't win. That's what you're saying?"

"I'm not saying anything. Obviously, she said yes. Eventually."

"She said yes there on that bench."

"See, it was fine." Obviously Scarlett was just trying to backtrack.

"She said she knew this was temporary and we had our life in LA to look forward to. I know I should have given her beach, not bench."

"Ha! Clever." Scarlett reacted to his quip. "She's a little obsessed with LA." She slipped a hand to her mouth. "Sorry. I didn't mean that in a bad way."

"And here we are in Alaska." Gil gestured to the room. "What about you and Alan? After the big production, did you say yes right then?

"Just like I had practiced it."

"Ouch."

"I couldn't ruin the perfect event, could I?"

Gil laughed at that, her wry sense of humor not lost on him. Time passed in silence while she busied herself with another granola bar and he grabbed his dad's book to add to the box. He ran his finger over the spines of another shelf of books, but he watched her too, stealing glances in her direction, wondering about an ability to make light, even of things that troubled her.

"You're not a Scrooge, Scarlett." The sudden thought transformed into words and came out of his mouth without warning.

"Thank you, Gil." She dropped wrappers into the wastebasket, then perched at the end of the desk. "You've only been stuck with me in an office for less than two hours though, so you might want to withhold judgment. Get me around some tinsel and a few Christmas carols and I might just lose it."

He remembered laughing with his sister, Izzy, over a line in a chick flick late one Friday night. "At least they haven't called you 'the only living heart donor,'" he said.

She looked at him strangely.

"Have they?" he stared at her.

"No." She raised her shoulders in his direction. "I'm just curious why you're quoting *Sabrina*. That's what they said about Harrison Ford's character."

"Blame my sister. She made me watch it one night after a date stood her up. He got what he wanted in the end, right?"

"True, but maybe I am like him. Putting money and business before love." She returned to recline into the chair before covering a yawn with her hand. "Been a long day."

"Wishing our buddies, Tyler and Rocky, hadn't taken the futon, aren't you?"

"That is morbid, Doctor. How can you joke about it?"

"Sorry. I'm tired too. Had an early start at the station with Cari."

"Is Cari short for Carole?"

He pointed at her. "We'll go with that answer."

Scarlett cocked her head but didn't say anything.

He studied her a moment too. "Mind if I ask a personal question?" he ventured.

"Looks like we're here all night. We might as well start in on the personal questions at some point. Now if it's what color is my toothbrush, that's personal, but I will answer it. Yellow." She raised her eyebrows with her smile, then leaned back on the seat and closed her eyes. "That's a very long way of saying go for it and see what happens."

"So I might find out something interesting like the color of your toothbrush?" He inserted some drama to his voice. "Will I be able to blackmail you with this information later on?"

"Maybe. Now what's your personal question?"

"You've been apart from Alan since . . . since . . . ?"

Scarlett opened her eyes. "July."

"Okay, since July. Absence makes the heart grow . . . what? Fill in the blank."

"Fill in the blank?" She scrunched her nose with the question.

"Don't think about it, just answer. Is it grow fonder or wander?" Moments passed as she slowly spun once in the chair with eyes closed as if she were meditating. She was going to take her time despite what he'd said.

The chair stopped. "Wonder. Absence makes the heart wonder." She paused before continuing. "Am I looking forward to going home because of Alan or because of the weather in Phoenix? It's a question I've begun to ask myself when I wake in the middle of the night because I'm freezing and need another blanket, or three."

"That's a blackmail-worthy answer."

"Just by you asking the question I think I've got some ammunition myself. How do you fill in the blank, Dr. Pennington the second?"

He took up his position at the edge of the desk. "Your answer seems to fit."

CHAPTER 7
Anchorage: 32°
Phoenix: 67°

Scarlett woke to animated voices and the clatter of desks unstacked and dragged from the doorway. Through bleary eyes she perceived Gil helping, pushing from inside the room. She fluffed what must have been a mess of curls by now and joined him as a couple of police officers pulled away the last of the barrier.

"Hey, look, Scarlett. You're no longer a hostage," Gil said when he saw her.

The officers exchanged glances and then looked hard at her. She covered a yawn, suddenly concerned about streaking mascara and sleep breath. "He's kidding. It was a joke from before." When they didn't crack a smile, she turned away to scrub under her eyes and run her tongue over her teeth and lips. This would have been a good time to have a stick of gum handy.

Their rescuers left, but a slight awkwardness descended, in contrast to the banter of comparing proposal stories and watching for one outside the window.

Darlene had finally looked at her phone about 10:30, after a play and late dinner with friends. She promised to call the moving company in the morning and file a complaint. According to Gil, Scarlett had fallen asleep around ten on the chair, with his jacket tucked under her head for a pillow.

She checked the time on her phone. *Way past time for*

anyone to get engaged. "Did I miss everything?"

"I missed it too. They finally showed up, but then I felt uncomfortable watching something so private."

"So private that they're going to be posting it online in the morning," she replied. He laughed with her, and then they both yawned. "I guess it's no fun being a stalker all by yourself."

"Right," he said.

She picked up his coat and held it out to him. "Thanks for this. Especially because it's freezing in here." She wrapped her arms across her chest. "Hope she said yes," she said through another yawn.

"Me too," replied Gil. "Are you going to be okay driving home? I'd offer you my couch, but I don't have one."

"If that's another crack about the futon, just stop it."

He held up his hands. "No, no. I meant at the hotel."

Scarlett wanted to ask about Carole. Maybe once she fell asleep he furiously texted his fiancée his annoyance at being stuck with a strange, chatty girl all evening. But Dr. Gilbert Taylor Pennington the Second's love life was none of her concern. She had her own to worry about, to wonder about. Gil's fill-in-the-blank question. It haunted her as she made the drive from Wasilla to her apartment in Anchorage. She had missed Alan's two calls and a text. She would reply to them in the morning.

Her stop for a sandwich and caffeine in the outskirts of the city helped her stay awake. She thought about Gil sliding the box of books into her back seat, apologizing the whole time for ruining her night. She had been the one to annoy the movers, but he was nice enough not to point that out. He even scraped her windshield. Fortunately the snowfall was light and the roads clear, but he waited for her to leave the parking lot and drive away. In the extreme cold. With no hat or gloves.

❄

After ignoring the alarm too many times, Scarlett hauled herself into the shower. Her first thought was of Gil and the books still in a box in the car. Maybe after such a crazy, late night she would stay home and read instead of driving in to the office. She looked outside to see if snow-covered roads might bolster the excuse, but no new snow had fallen. The roads were as clear as when she came back from the college. A text from Trina forced her decision. *Where are you? I have news.*

She wanted to text back and ask if Marley had died, but instead she replied, *On my way.*

When the elevator doors opened, Scarlett noticed the plastic jack-o'-lantern gracing the top of the lobby Christmas tree. Finally an attempt, albeit a small one, to get holidays straight. As she followed the garland, she began to hum "O Christmas Tree," forming new words in her head to a verse involving witches and ghosts.

Hannah jumped up from Scarlett's chair where she had been waiting to pounce. "Glenda said North Pole is out. She heard about Micki and the Dickens Village."

"What? Just yesterday she faxed her agreement." Scarlett pulled off her cap and smoothed down flyaways. She'd flat ironed her hair too quickly that morning.

"You should go see her. She's much better to deal with in person," Hannah said.

Anything had to be better than their phone conversations. "I can go Wednesday. Do you think she'll let me make an appointment, though? I don't want to go and have her refuse to see me."

"I can call her for you. Act like a secretary scheduling your appointments."

What happened to Hannah, and who was this new person in her place? "Sure. You seem to know her." Scarlett pulled out her phone, checked her schedule, and frowned. "I'll be at KWIX in the morning. How long does it take to drive to North Pole?"

"It's like six hours," Trina chimed in.

"Can you ask her if 4:00 would work?" Scarlett would have a long drive back home that evening, but saving the sponsorship would be worth it. She'd pack an overnight bag and book a hotel room just in case.

"I'll tell her you're coming and what time."

Maybe that was where Scarlett had gone wrong with convincing North Pole to sign on as a sponsor. Instead of asking if the town wanted to be involved, she should have told their mayor the Christmas spirit campaign depended on their support. Because it was true. And no one in the office let her forget it.

Except North Pole didn't have a Christmas spirit problem. That was Glenda Sprouse's standard line on the phone the few times they'd spoken.

So Scarlett would sit down with her and talk about promoting Alaska at Christmastime. She would explain again that sponsors would appear on all the publicity whether it was the radio spots or the entry forms to win an Alaskan adventure vacation.

"One more thing." Hannah lingered for a reason. "What would you think about scheduling my mom's Dickens carolers?"

Scarlett already had carolers, but maybe Hannah was offended because her mom's company hadn't been asked. "Of course, that'd be great. Thanks for thinking of it."

After Hannah left, Scarlett found Trina watching her. "What?"

"You told me you were going straight to the community college from work, and then today Daniel said you didn't make it back until midnight. It's not even an hour's drive. I'm no Sherlock, but that can only mean you were with Dr. Gravy the whole time."

Soon Scarlett had spilled the whole story. "And now I'm wondering about Alan even more, and I feel terrible."

"You don't look like you feel terrible. Unless I'm misreading your smile."

"I'm not smiling." Her phone buzzed with a text. The number began with an unfamiliar area code. *Make it home okay last night?* A second, but completely unnecessary text popped up. *This is Gil, BTW.*

She knew immediately. After all, who else had she been with last night? Her eyes widened. "It's from him."

"Gravy? And no, you're right. You're not smiling at all."

"Trina, what am I going to do?" Scarlett flopped into her seat. "What happened to 'I'm taken, he's taken'? It keeps my life simpler. I can work and not be distracted, then go home, start Ambrose Events, and plan a wedding to Alan Blankenship, who loves me and wants to marry me. At least that's what he keeps saying." She spun in her office chair. "I don't know what I want

CHRISTMAS FUTURE

anymore. How can I believe anything after what Lexi did?"

"You mean what's-her-name?" Trina jibed. She grabbed the sides of Scarlett's seat to stop the spinning. "Listen to me. Forget about Gravy. You had your fling, stuck in an English professor's office half the night with a gorgeous doctor. I don't feel sorry for you, by the way, but mark it off your bucket list and stick with reality. You'll be gone in a month, and he'll probably be gone next week."

The words penetrated, causing her still-spinning thoughts to slow. "That's the most mature thing I've heard you say, Trina. Thank you. I needed that."

"Do you want me to slap you twice across the face?"

"No, why would I want that?"

"They do it in the movies when they want to knock some sense into somebody."

"I take back what I said about you being mature. But I will face reality. Alan asked me to fly home this weekend to attend a dinner because he's receiving an award for work. I told him no because if I stay busy here I can be done sooner and come home sooner, but I think I'll go. I need to. It's the mature thing to do."

"I'm so glad you figured out your love life because look who has news?" She waved her left hand.

"Please don't slap me."

"Scarlett, ring on my finger news!" She wiggled her third finger, where a small diamond sparkled.

Scarlett scooped up Trina's hand for inspection. "Heath proposed? I didn't know you were getting that close." In between work phone calls and emails, she and Trina discussed wedding dates and dresses, cakes and flowers, and a myriad of other matrimonial particulars. She would have gotten more work done if she'd stayed home and read, but Daniel wouldn't have to know that.

Around 11:30, Trina got up to leave for an early lunch with Heath but lingered at the opening to the cubicle. "We haven't set a date, but I'd love it if somehow you could come, Scarlett."

"Make it a summer wedding, and I'm here."

Trina sighed the sigh of the newly engaged. "Summer would be perfect. I want to get married in Seward at the red church where my gramps was priest before he died. Growing up, my grandparents' house was my favorite place in the summer."

Once Scarlett was alone, she booked a flight to Phoenix, then texted Alan about her change of plans. She also texted her parents and her sister, telling them she'd be there for Halloween. The thought of home warmed her clear to her bones as she made mental plans for trick-or-treating with her two nieces. She'd make Alan go too.

Daniel leaned his head over the low wall. "Sorry you got stuck in Wasilla. We didn't even get that much snow down here." He'd assumed getting home so late was due to the weather, and that was fine with her.

"It all worked out, and now I've got plenty of reference material." They discussed the project a bit, but her mind was on her planned trip to Arizona. Maybe she should have mentioned it to him before making it official, but too late. "Daniel, I have to go to Phoenix at the end of the week, but the flight leaves early Friday. Is that a problem?"

"Shouldn't be, as long as everything gets done in time. Meant to tell you, I promised my sister that we'd book her neighbor's group, the Charles Dickens Carolers."

"I have a company supplying carolers. Actually two."

"Now you have one more." Daniel continued toward the elevators for his lunch break.

Fine. Whatever. Scarlett checked her phone. Her sister had texted several smiley faces, a row of thumbs ups, and one jack-o'-lantern emoji. Her mom said *Great*! Dad said *Can't wait to see you.* Alan hadn't responded yet. She clicked on Gil's message. She really should reply to it. At least say yes, she made it. Say thanks for asking. Hope you got some sleep. Something. Just to be polite.

She studied his two brief texts, considering what might be most appropriate. Something light, simple. To the point.

The drive home was fine. Thanks for the books. Boring as far as texts go but he had asked a straightforward question, so brevity was probably called for.

A near-immediate return text surprised her. *I made it back to my dad's office. You'll be happy to know that the desks and the movers are gone. Glad I got here late enough to miss them.*

He was kind not to include an emoji or two to express how

he really felt about their evening stuck together. Certainly he was happy to be done with the girl who begged for books and yelled at furniture movers who were only doing their job. She reread the text, wondering if guys even sent emojis. Alan didn't. She contemplated her reply. *Y-a-y.* Lame. She deleted each letter and instead went with: *Tread lightly. I wouldn't trust T and R.*

Good point was his return text.

Scarlett pushed the phone out of her line of sight. She'd skipped breakfast, and her grumbling stomach wouldn't let her disregard lunch as well. She required food and then had a full afternoon of work to do. Especially because she was taking Friday off.

Maybe one more text. Just because she was curious. She reached for her phone.

Scarlett: *My coworker Trina just got engaged. He hid the ring in a treasure chest she added to her aquarium and he was standing behind her to pop the question. Thumbs up/thumbs down?*

Gil: *Did his proposal include the phrase "out of all the fish in the sea"?*

Scarlett: *I cannot confirm or deny*

Gil: *A+ for cheesy. Or would that be a D- for cheesy? Cheese is fish bait.*

Scarlett: *But A+ for creativity?*

Gil: *Maybe*

Scarlett: *Does it help knowing that he runs a pet store with her uncle and she's been buying fish from him for over a year?*

Gil: *Ah. The personal, familial angle.*

Scarlett: *No one uses the word familial in a text*

Gil: *You just did.*

Scarlett: *You must be the son of an English professor*

Gil: *Does it show?*

Scarlett: *With every bit of punctuation Is it killing you that I didn't put a period right there?*

Gil: *Not really.*

Scarlett: *Liar*

Gil: *.*

Scarlett: *!*

Gil: *I didn't see a fish tank in the quad last night.*

Scarlett: *Excellent observation. I double-checked that Trina and Heath were not that couple.*

Their texting conversation lasted through what should have been her lunch break, forcing her to scavenge from the vending machine and work with practically one eye on her phone the whole time. No small feat since she was trying to keep the Gil-conversation from Trina, who had returned from her hour with Heath in a blissful flurry before announcing that she was leaving for the day. Apparently to go dress shopping.

Scarlett could relate to Trina's euphoria, but her own post-proposal bliss had been extremely short-lived. She'd said yes to Alan when he popped the question on Christmas Eve, and then two hours later she received a low-balance alert to her phone from the bank. Low-balance really meant no balance. And all compliments of Lexi Bloom.

She finally dropped her phone into her purse. She didn't want to think about Lexi, and she didn't need to keep texting Gil. She had to work. Finally she retrieved a couple of Gil's dad's books out of her car to lose herself in the Victorian world of nineteenth-century London.

CHAPTER 8
Anchorage: 46°
Los Angeles: 84°

Wonder? Wander? Grow fonder?

Once Gil finally got going for the day, he'd racked his memory, trying to figure out where his ridiculous fill in the blank question came from. It was what kept him awake in his hotel room after campus security freed them from the desk blockade and he saw Scarlett off in the parking lot. He finally crawled into bed after midnight but that didn't mean his thoughts stopped whirling. Had the question been lurking in the shadows of his brain all these months when he was a busy doctor and seeing Cari only on weekends? And not even every weekend because he diligently took his turn on call once a month.

But then he'd admitted that "wonder" seemed an appropriate response. It came out in the way he implored Scarlett, "Don't think about it, just answer."

He set his phone on the desk. No more texting. He was here to pack up, not discuss marriage proposals with a girl he just met last week. Cari had cancelled dinner plans due to meetings running late at KWIX which would allow him to work uninterrupted. He could subsist on the leftover granola bars. That was why he bought them.

But texting was more enjoyable than reading book titles. There were so many, shelf after shelf of them, and he hoped the university library would be interested in increasing their fiction and nonfiction collections. Otherwise, he needed help carting them off to a local nonprofit.

When he'd boxed up the majority of them, he carried the two his dad authored over to the desk and relaxed into the chair. These would go to the college library as well since he and Izzy already had personalized copies. Scarlett held the most recently published one, and the fourth waited on the computer in front of him. Recovering the manuscript should have been his top priority, but uncertainty about his dad's wishes lingered. He and Izzy didn't even know he'd been writing again or if he planned to switch publishers. She said to sell to the one that had been calling. Maybe she was right. The money could pay off her and her husband's student loans and even provide college funds for Penn and Ember.

He retrieved his phone and selected the secretary's number. "Darlene? This is Gil. I need a computer hack. Is there an IT department on campus that might bypass my dad's password?" After taking down the information, including directions for finding the right building, he made another call. This time to the London publisher who would be pleased with the message he received on his voicemail. "I'll contact you as soon as I have the manuscript off my dad's hard drive," he said into his phone.

He dusted off the computer case and disconnected all the cables before snagging his coat. Still so much to do in his dad's office, but a brisk walk between buildings sounded appealing. He dug around in a pile of outerwear stuffed in a low desk drawer and procured a fur-lined leather cap of sorts. Alaskan brisk was a far cry from southern California anything. Even with the sun out, extra warmth was called for.

The soggy remains of the late-night proposal stuck to his boots as he traversed the quad. So much for all those rose petals. He adjusted his load onto his left side, thinking he might pull out his phone to send Scarlett a picture of the aftermath. He changed his mind.

Let it go.

But his mind wandered . . . the scene outside the office window when the couple finally made their appearance, the way they snuggled and kissed and laughed before the guy got down on one knee . . . and the scene inside, when Scarlett curled up on his coat on the chair and fell into a deep sleep. He stopped watching the couple at the actual moment of popping the question, but watching Scarlett sleep felt intimate as well. They barely knew each other, yet somehow being stuck together for an evening had a way of advancing a relationship.

Gil opened the door to the computer science building, where he quickly found the IT lab.

"Dude, you're trailing petals. You're a freaking flower girl." The guy behind the counter spoke before Gil even had a chance to set down the computer.

"They're all over the quad."

"I swear there's a proposal at least every other month out there. I was here late anyway, but I heard some guy and his angry girlfriend got stuck in one of the offices in the . . . was it the English department? Yeah. The girl teed off the furniture guys and they piled up—"

"I heard about it," Gil interrupted. "Look, I've got a hard drive that I need to get data off of. Is there someone who can do that?"

"Yeah, sure. Can you leave it overnight?"

"No problem."

The kid shuffled among the parts and tools that littered the workspace before producing a pad of sticky notes. "What department are you from?"

He had to ask. "Uh, Darlene Maxfield sent me."

"Love Darlene." He scribbled something then pushed the colored square across the counter. "Here. Write down your number."

Gil added his name as well and passed it back.

"Whoa. Pennington. Dude, you're not Dr. P's son, are you?" He shook a finger in the direction of Gil's head. "When I saw that hat, I wondered there for a second, but I was like, nah."

"You knew my dad?" Somehow Gil hadn't considered that his dad would have known more than just the department secretary. He spent two years on campus. Obviously he would have friends and acquaintances.

"Are you kidding? He's the only reason I made it through freshman English. That man is a saint, well"—his tone slowed—"was a saint. I'm sorry. You gotta know he's really missed around here." He patted the hard drive. "I know this computer. Your dad, he knew his similes and metaphors, but computers? Not all that much."

Gil laughed, but warmth flooded his chest at the mention of his dad. "That's him," he managed to say.

"It's a miracle I even remember what a simile and a metaphor are." He pressed the sticky note to the drive. "So, dude, where's your favorite fishing spot with your dad?"

"Fishing spot?"

"Yeah, here in Alaska. Innoka, Kenai, or maybe Bristol Bay? One time on the Kenai River we . . ."

"You fished with my dad?"

"Heck, yeah. He and the head of the department fished sometimes, so they'd invite a couple of us from IT." His eyes lost focus for a moment, as if he was remembering. "Oh, he told me you were in med school or something."

"By the time he was up here I had finished school and was working in California paying off a contract. If I'd known about his health, though, I would have figured something out. You know, come."

"Sure, sure, of course. No judgment here, but he talked about you, man. You were a doctor. You were helping poor people. And, I think, a grandson?"

"My sister's."

"But you got engaged, right? And I remember when the baby was born. Dr. P was so happy about that. Whoa, then I remember he went to visit that summer, like, was it . . . um . . . Spo-kane?" He struggled to pronounce it.

"Yeah, we met at my sister's there in the summer and always at Christmas. He'd come down and I'd fly up." Gil let out a slow, calming breath. "You don't know how good it feels to talk to someone who knew my dad." Except for the stark reminder that Gil had never visited him in Alaska.

The guy stood abruptly and walked to a shelf in the corner. He returned holding a framed picture. "Check this out. Our last fishing trip. He said it's where he used to go with his dad and his brothers."

"You're kidding." The information settled on Gil's chest like a solid warm hug or a brawny football player's block. He wasn't sure which impression lingered more heavily. "Where was this taken?"

"The Chena River. Runs through Fairbanks. One of his old buddies met us, some guy. He had a weird name. Ves, Vester?"

"Thanks for your help. Sorry, I didn't catch your name." He hadn't meant to take up the guy's time.

"Nate."

"Thank you, Nate. I appreciate hearing about my dad, and I'll wait till you call about the data."

"Will do."

Gil didn't return to his dad's office. Instead, he headed for the parking lot because a new idea was forming. One that involved a road trip. He called Cari. "Do you want to take a drive? I'm thinking about going to Fairbanks."

She waited a beat before answering with a question. "Tonight?"

"Right now."

He heard a muffled, "Where's Fairbanks?" then Cari's voice louder again. "Gil, Fairbanks is six hours away."

"So we'll stay overnight."

"Are you saying you're done with your dad's office? You can fly home with me?"

The word "home" struck him. The closest thing he had was his hotel room a block from the college. His parents' house had been sold, and his dad had moved north within six months of his mother's passing. Izzy pleaded with Dad to move close to her in Eastern Washington, but when a chance to teach English presented itself, end of discussion. "My home's gone," Dad said. "So I think I'll go back home." He and his sister knew Dad meant Mom, not the house. And back home was Alaska.

Gil cleared out his own condo in Riverside before flying up to do the same to his dad's office. He was living out of a suitcase and sleeping on a rented bed. He didn't call LA home, but neither was anywhere else.

"We're flying back to Cali at the end of the week, right, Gil?" Cari tried again to fish for an answer.

He lingered inside the double doors at the entrance of the college, monitoring how the whitening sky blocked out the sun. A hint of snow swirled, and he prepared to brave the cold again.

He wouldn't tell her that the office was still undone. How he accomplished nothing last night after she left. He would skip any mention of being stuck there until after ten, the subsequent sleeping in, and the text-fest with Scarlett.

"I think I need more time," he said. Apparently for a lot of things. "But you'll be happy because I just dropped off my dad's computer at the tech department. Soon I'll have his manuscript to submit to that publisher."

"So did you call them?"

"I left a message."

Her squeal penetrated the air waves before he continued.

"So what do you think about Fairbanks? The thing is I don't know how long it's going to take for someone to do their hack job, so why not visit my dad's hometown while I wait?"

Cari's end of the line was quiet for too long. "Are you okay?" she finally asked.

He let out a long breath. "I don't know. Why?" She was quiet again, so he continued. "All I know is that up until last week I was working ten or twelve hours a day, and now I'm tossing books into boxes. It feels off."

"No, I know what it is. You're just grieving your dad's death and feeling bad because you hardly saw him the last couple years of his life."

"Thanks for the reminder." He'd just been hit with that, but it wasn't the tech guy's fault. Cari, though, could have stopped after "grieving dad's death."

"Seriously, Gil. Going to Fairbanks will only make it worse. Do you know what you need? Los Angeles! I know you told them you'd join the team in January, but move it up. It's not good for you not to be busy. You just said so."

"What are you going to do?"

"I have a few more meetings with Hudson, and the crew. Then I'm out of here. Have you noticed, it's freezing? I have to figure out some better outerwear for when I come back to record the TV segments."

After goodbyes and I love yous, Gil pulled at the hat he wore, his dad's hat, then climbed into the rental to start the engine. The vents full-blasted him, so he knocked the heater down a few notches till it could warm up. He played with the

CHRISTMAS FUTURE

GPS, still considering Fairbanks.

    Had she paused after saying Hudson's name, before tacking on "the crew," or was he imagining it? Had she wandered because they spent so much time apart? *What about us?* he wanted to ask, but maybe that wasn't a conversation to have over the phone.

CHAPTER 9
Anchorage: 40°
Phoenix: 90°

After her immersion in revival architecture, corsets and crinolines, and pea-souper London fog, emphasis on the fog, Scarlett mentally allowed herself to reenter the real world of the four manufactured walls of her cubicle. Trina's absence from the office had given Scarlett the quiet she needed to Google every Victorian, Dickens, Old World, Ye Olde Days of Yore kind of Christmas village that existed in the entire contiguous forty-eight states and Hawaii. That was only after skim-reading what she'd borrowed from the late Professor Pennington. The reference material had painted both a picture of Dickensian charm and a disgusting depiction of life in London's pitiable underbelly. She'd been forced back online in an effort to simplify.

After pages of notes, she settled on a rough outline that drew from both. She had a plan to wow Mayor Blanding, the governor, and anyone else who cared. And tomorrow she would sit down with the mayor of North Pole to seal that deal again.

In the middle of her new to-do list she received a call from Daniel. "Hey, be over at the TV station by 4:00. They want to sketch out your segments before Christmas Carole flies out. I'll email notes."

"Am I off the hook for the meeting tomorrow morning?"

"They didn't say."

She made a mental note to give the station her phone number so she could accept or reject their demands as needed

CHRISTMAS FUTURE

because no one who valued the parameters of an eight-hour workday scheduled meetings for 4:00. If they canceled tomorrow, though, there would be no complaints from her. Even the drive to KWIX today put her halfway home. After a stop at Ruby's for some overdue Tomato Basil, of course.

In her hierarchy of thoughts, though, soup and phone numbers didn't make the top. Gil did. *Because of the books.* That's what she told herself anyway. If Carole was flying out, he was too. Unfortunately she had no time for a quick trip to Wasilla to return what she borrowed, so she'd take them with her to the station and hope he showed up there before leaving the state.

After removing each sticky note poking out of every book, she stacked them up and reached for her coat. She repeated her morning ritual in reverse. Coat, scarf, gloves, hat. What had Trina said, something about reality? Here was reality: Gil going back to his life with Carole in LA. She going back to Arizona to reconnect with Alan. Everything back to normal.

While navigating the streets to central Anchorage, Scarlett silently cursed the thermometer. Before warming up, the heater blasted cold as if she needed the reminder: time to invest in a new outerwear wardrobe. She'd been getting by with her fall choice of coats, but her inner core was begging *please, please, please* for something with a lower temperature rating than hers currently provided.

Soon the gray-blue building loomed and she found the parking structure easily. Her email included a printable pass that allowed her into the VIP section. Quick in and out. *Perfect.* She arrived at the front desk at five minutes to four, refusing to be the reason anyone worked late. Including herself. At every stoplight she had perused the notes on her phone. She planned for the meeting itself to also be a quick in and out.

An assistant with a lanyard ID and a clipboard showed her to the studio with instructions to "wait right here," but after he exited, Scarlett couldn't help but plant herself in front of the set. The understated, but eye-catching baubles and greenery drew her in. She'd been in reluctant-Christmas mode since July, but this took her breath away. A lush evergreen wrapped with traditional red and gold lights and trim brushed the ceiling in one corner.

Whimsical rough-cut figurines of bears, moose, and wolves, made festive with colorful ribbons, greeted her at every turn, while berry and bough wreaths adorned the window panes on three walls.

The look, pulled straight out of the Alaskan wilderness, somehow achieved an elegance and appeal that she wouldn't have thought possible. A faint scent of pine drifted her way, clearly from some sort of plug-in and not the artificial tree. Maybe she would have to seek out the set decorator for help creating the Dickens masterpiece she had planned.

"Excuse me," the assistant interrupted. "Hudson's running late, so he said just throw the meeting back on Wednesday's calendar."

Scarlett's hope for tomorrow deflated a bit. "Turns out my schedule's going to be pretty tight. Can I trust 8:30 a.m. still works for him?"

"Definitely. Hudson's good about that kind of thing." He smiled as if the current situation didn't just prove otherwise.

Scarlett lingered, hoping to take one last look at the set. "I guess this is for Christmas Carole?" She waved a hand toward it.

"Just the mock-up, not the final or anything. Actually the art department probably doesn't want anyone seeing it yet."

"But it's gorgeous."

"They're perfectionists. They'll add in details that will blow your mind."

Scarlett must have paused too long, because he said, "This way, please," and escorted her to the lobby. Her stop at Ruby's would come a little earlier than planned.

Once back in the parking garage, she slipped into her car and pulled the door shut. She knocked the heat down a few notches to give it time to warm up then reached for her phone to call in the soup order. The noise of a fancy black SUV caught her attention as it claimed a reserved spot in front of the main entrance, and the doors opened to reveal a smartly dressed couple. Hudson and Carole.

Scarlett shrunk down slightly in her seat to watch unnoticed. She was both annoyed that the producer would cancel a meeting as quickly as he had called for one, and insulted on Gil's behalf that the reason might involve his own fiancée. As they paused to laugh and talk, Scarlett's indignation got the better of her. She revved her engine, reversed her way out of the parking spot, and glided past, making sure she was recognized.

On the drive to Ruby's she purposely turned up the radio in an effort to drown out thoughts of Mr. KWIX and Christmas Carole. They'd appeared a little startled when they noticed her, but hopefully they realized how rude they were to not show up for the impromptu meeting. With her car barely warmed up, she pulled into the parking lot, sorry that she had been interrupted before making the call for curb-side service. She huddled into her coat a little tighter and entered the restaurant to snag the end of the line.

A kid that was all skinny jeans and blond, bristly hair approached her. "Scarlett? I'm Heath. Remember we were at the thing."

Trina's Heath? "Oh, right. Though I don't think we actually met. More like saw each other across the parking lot."

"I've got good eyes, and I definitely remember you." His brows rose with his comment.

Mentally, she cringed. If he meant the remark as a compliment, it sure didn't feel like one. "Congratulations on your engagement."

"I texted you about that. I hope it's okay that Trina gave me your number."

Scarlett palmed her phone. "Sorry, I must have missed it." She pulled off a glove to flip through until she found his message. "An engagement party?"

"I know you're an event planner. Trina told me. She also said you're busy all the time with work stuff, but I just need help with Hawaiian food and plates and silverware and stuff."

"Nice choice. She loves all things Hawaii."

"That's why I'm surprising her with tickets to get married there. I can't wait to see her face when she—"

Married there? "Heath, wait. Have you talked to her about venues?"

"Venues? What's that?"

"Like where the ceremony will take place."

"On the beach, duh."

"You should discuss this with her."

"That would spoil the surprise. I thought maybe Sunday night would be good."

Scarlett envied his enthusiasm, but it wouldn't last when he found out that Trina had her heart set on Seward not sand. "Sunday won't work for me. I'm going to Arizona for the weekend. I really think you should talk to Trina, though. How about when I get back, I sit down with both of you?"

"I guess I can wait, but next week for sure. And I think you're talking about the red church thing. That's nothing compared to the beach."

He knew and he didn't care. She grasped his arm and forced eye contact. "Heath, don't buy any tickets or make any reservations until I get back."

Like she didn't have anything else to do but plan engagement parties and mediate wedding plans. Only everything she was already behind on, compounded by the fact that she'd be out of the office Friday.

Friday. She looked forward to a grand thawing out that would begin at exactly 4:36 when she got off the plane in 90 degree weather. Nothing else mattered.

At home, Scarlett carried the soup and foil-wrapped breadsticks to the chair closest to the space heater in her small living room. She didn't have the nerve to attempt a fire in the fireplace, but the heater and a thick quilt defrosted the day's chill well enough. Professor Pennington's *Dickens at Christmas* and a few of his other books were stacked on a side table, in case she wanted to do one last flip through.

Savoring the Tomato Basil, she replayed her conversation with Heath. She needed to make him understand what Trina really wanted. That loving someone was in the details. Her eyes lingered on the stack of borrowed books. Maybe she could text Gil. Only the night before they'd had a conversation about proposals, followed by a text thread that day specifically about Heath's proposal to Trina. He'd understand.

She hesitated, tapping her fingers across the screen of her phone. She texted with him way too much already. He was going to think she was a stalker. One appeared from Heath. *What do you think about hula dancers?*

She tapped her phone back on and found Gil's number near

CHRISTMAS FUTURE

the top of her messages, just under Alan's reply to the news that she was coming for the weekend. Alan wouldn't care about Trina and Heath. Besides he'd mentioned an early meeting the next day. He wouldn't appreciate a late phone call or text.

She selected Gil's name. *I have a question. Got a minute?*

❄

Scarlett woke with chattering teeth in the frigid, darkened living room. The space heater had timed out, and she was pretty sure she would see her breath, if she could see at all. Ignoring the stiffness in her neck she leaned down to feel for the quilt that had fallen off as she slept. Once cocooned inside, she waddled over to restart the heater. Her more comfortable bed sat only steps away in the next room, but that would mean moving the heater too, and she just didn't have the energy. The couch would do.

Soon her eyes drooped onto a scene of a large-mouthed fish coming straight for her, its humongous black eyes drilling deeper and deeper, and Trina's voice, "Marley's dead."

Scarlett blinked herself awake. The first bits of day materialized around the wood blinds at her window. What time was it? She had an 8:30 meeting. She snatched up her phone and headed to the bathroom for a shower. She couldn't be late. She was supposed to meet Glenda in North Pole at four, so she absolutely had to be done at KWIX and on her way before ten.

While waiting for her drive-thru coffee, she texted Trina. *Keep Marley out of my dreams.*

No response from Gil to her question last night. She must have used up her quota of texts to guys that were engaged to someone else. With a few clicks she deleted their entire conversation.

❄ ❄ ❄

Anchorage: 40°
Los Angeles: 81°

The towering evergreens lining both sides of the road

scraped the white sky, creating an ethereal, almost otherworldly feel as Gil approached the highway. Only ruined by the heater that still breathed cold, of course. He took the ramp south toward Anchorage instead of following the GPS he set yesterday. Because of the worsening weather, and maybe partly due to Cari's words yesterday, he abandoned plans to drive up to Fairbanks. Instead he would be at the TV station this morning when she finished her final meeting to drive her to the airport. She had decided not to wait for him to finish the mess in the office, as she described it. Certainly settling on a publisher for the Dickens manuscript played a part in her decision. It seemed to be what she cared about.

He hugged the right lane, prepared to take it slow in the patchy fog as he allowed his mind to wander. His Alaskan adventure with Cari had failed to live up to his expectations. He had known they would both be busy, her on plans for the Christmas show and him with packing his dad's things, but they spent as much time apart as together. And Cari wasn't complaining about it. Of course, maybe he wasn't either. *Are we already so used to focusing on work? Is that any way to start a marriage?* The questions broadsided him. He reeled his thoughts back. She was building her television career while he had been entrenched in his medical practice. They were supporting each other. They had an understanding. Nothing wrong with that.

They'd had fun in college—late nights studying, hiking and hanging out with friends on the weekends, and sneaking off for an hour's drive to the beach as often as possible. Again, there was nothing wrong with facing reality and getting serious about their careers. That's what people did in their late twenties.

It doesn't have to be that way. The thought popped into his head without warning, followed immediately by an image of his parents. Their marriage wasn't perfect, but they seemed to want to be together, even up until the end. In fact, never more than at the end.

Gil pulled at his dad's fur-lined hat, grateful for its warmth. Scarlett had said something about starting a marriage in debt. At least he and Cari wouldn't have that problem.

CHAPTER 10
Anchorage: 31°
Phoenix: 88°

Scarlett waited at KWIX, watching the minutes tick by on her phone. At 9:15 she approached the desk again. "Have you heard anything from Hudson yet?"

The receptionist paused noticeably before repeating herself. "I'm sorry, no," she said, then added, "That's how these things are. A lot of hurry up and wait, I'm afraid."

"But I have an appointment in North Pole." Scarlett definitely needed more hurry. Maybe bringing up North Pole was a mistake, making it seem less critical than it truly was. She was not on her way to sit on Santa's knee. She had a crisis to avert.

The woman's eyes glazed slightly at the mention of the appointment again. "Would you like to wait in the studio?" she offered finally.

The same assistant from yesterday escorted Scarlett inside, where she immediately tiptoed toward the set to observe. It remained much the same as before except for the scattering of set designers filling shelves with wood plates and texture-glazed pottery.

"Hey, what are you doing here?"

She turned at the sound of Gil's voice approaching from the shadows. As he appeared at her left, she scrambled for a witty reply but came up empty. "Probably waiting for the same people you are," she offered lamely.

75

"Waiting seems to be the name of the game around here."

Scarlett nodded her agreement. "I heard you're leaving town, but I still have your dad's books."

"Why don't you keep them? I'm donating them to the college library anyway."

"What about—" Scarlett's phone rang. She quickly checked the screen. "Sorry. I need to answer this. Hi, Trina."

"You told me to call you by 9:30. Time to leave for North Pole."

"Thank you." She turned away from Gil's view and lowered her tone. "Can you believe they haven't even shown up?"

"You have to go, Scarlett. Right now."

"I know."

"Why are you being so quiet?"

Only one word of explanation came to mind. "Gravy," she mumbled. She spun back around. "Talk to you later, okay?" She ended the call and slid the phone into her purse. "I have to go."

"Is something wrong?" Gil looked genuinely concerned.

"I have a schedule. Apparently some people don't know what that means, you know, to be where you say you're going to be at a certain time. You can tell them that when you see them." She bit back her resentment. *I shouldn't take this out on him.*

"Scarlett! Thank you for waiting." Hudson's voice boomed all the way to the pine bough wreaths and back. "I am so sorry. I got stuck on the phone."

"And wardrobe was a mess," came from Carole who was at his side. The assistant trailed them.

"I have to go," Scarlett shot back. Heat spiked up the back of her neck and across both cheeks. "I have an appointment. And I keep my appointments." She turned on her heel and strode from the studio, anxious to get away, and not only because she was late getting on the road to North Pole. She wished she had remained a bit calmer in front of Gil, but even the fact that she cared what he thought irritated her. He was flying out today. They'd never cross paths again.

As she marched to her car and locked herself inside, she imagined their conversation. *Was that really the woman in charge of increasing Christmas spirit?*

Thanks to VIP parking, she would have another quick in

and out, like yesterday, and maybe Daniel needed to find a replacement for her Christmas Carole segments. She turned the key, but the engine sputtered. After several attempts, it still wouldn't engage. She strangled the steering wheel with both hands. *Not a dead battery. Not today.*

She tried one more time before hearing a knock on her window and finding Gil in a hideous fur-lined hat gesturing and speaking a muffled, "Need help?"

Leave me to my misery. He was the last person she wanted to accept help from after her less-than-stellar performance in the studio.

He gestured for her to roll down the window, but when she pressed the button, nothing happened. She opened her car door. "My battery's dead, obviously. And what dead animal are you wearing on your head?"

"All I'm going to say is that my ears are warmer than yours. Look, I'd give you a jump start, but my car's out there with the non-VIPs." He pointed with his full arm extended. "Can I give you a ride to your appointment?"

"No. You can't." Her words might have come out too abruptly. Why was he so nice? Even while looking stupid in that hat.

"I don't mind. Really."

"Stop it. I have a six-hour drive, so don't tell me you don't mind."

"Where do you need to be?"

"North Pole. Now can I close my door? It's freezing." And her embarrassment was showing.

"I was thinking of going to Fairbanks anyway. It's on the way."

"You do not have to make up for Hudson being late."

"This back and forth isn't getting us anywhere except colder. And looks like it's starting to snow. You don't want to be driving in this."

Scarlett checked her phone. It was her drop-dead leave time. She absolutely could not miss her chance to fix things with Glenda.

Again, why was he so nice? Her outburst Monday night got them stuck in an office for hours. Certainly he didn't deserve to be confined in a car with her for even longer. But she wasn't going anywhere with a dead battery. A taxi? An Uber? A bus? They would take time she didn't have.

"Okay, but only if you let me pay for gas."

"Deal."

"And lose the hat."

He gave her a side-eye look, and soon they were on the road, begging for the heat to kick in and the snowfall to be light.

"You're stuck with me again. That's twice now. Rough week," she said without sarcasm.

He laughed anyway. "And you're my hostage again. Just remember you agreed to it this time."

Scarlett patted the passenger-side door. "But I have an escape hatch, if it comes to that." She smiled and reclined into her seat. She had questions for him but didn't want to pry so soon into their road trip. There were six long hours to learn why he was on the way to destinations north instead of on a plane with his fiancée to a much warmer LA. She pulled up notes on her tablet, claiming she had work to do. *He's taken,* she reminded herself. *I'm taken. We're all taken.*

❆

Scarlett stirred in the passenger seat, then attempted to stretch inconspicuously before collecting the tablet from near her feet. "I'm sorry I'm not much of a traveling companion." She covered a yawn.

"What are you talking about? The snoring was entertaining," Gil quipped. His hat was off. He must have warmed up enough.

"I do not snore." She smoothed her hair, resisting the urge to flip down the visor mirror to primp.

"That's what everyone says." He raised an eyebrow in her direction and then turned back to the road. "Apparently my talent is being so boring that it puts you to sleep."

"That's becoming a thing, isn't it?" She yawned again. "So I should blame you instead of my restless attempts at sleeping in a chair last night. Which is also becoming a thing." She adjusted the seat belt around her puffy coat. No reason to be embarrassed since he was right. He had already observed her sleeping once.

"Still another hour to the North Pole. Do you want to stop for lunch or wait until we get there?" he asked.

"You're always good for some granola bars, right?"

"Fresh out."

"My appointment's at four. Sorry I didn't plan time for eating." She didn't know she'd be sharing the ride.

"It must be important," he said.

"Thank you for saying that because every time I say North Pole, I get visions of long Christmas wish lists while sitting on Santa's knee. This is definitely work related and definitely a big deal."

"I got that impression at KWIX this morning."

Scarlett cringed. "Yeah. That. All part of my Scrooge mentality. Work, work, work. Time is money." The cringe continued all the way to her toes.

"So are you saying that you're going to the North Pole and not even going to see Santa Claus at all?"

"Quit saying *the* North Pole. It's just North Pole. You need to know this before we get there."

"North Pole. Got it. But you didn't answer my question. Don't you even want to take a drive down Santa Claus Lane?"

"This is serious, remember? If I don't have Mayor Sprouse and the town sponsoring the Christmas spirit campaign, I fail. If I don't deliver a Victorian Village that Mayor Blanding finds acceptable, I fail. But North Pole thinks a Victorian Village infringes on their brand." She pointed at him. "You find Santa and see if he can wrap all that up into a nice, neat package."

He nodded, and soon they settled into a comfortable silence as they traveled down the highway. Only scattered snowflakes fell, and the road remained clear. She focused on the idyllic scene around her. She'd never get used to the stark contrast of majestic, white-frosted evergreens and the bluest of blue rivers winding alongside them. Back in Arizona, the trees shared space with saguaro cactus and desert brown landscapes. Riverbeds ran dry with dust, not water.

She leaned forward in her seat. "Is that an eagle?"

Gil followed her gaze. "Yeah. Wow."

She put a hand to her mouth, awed by the grandeur of the

bird's effortless flight. She craned her neck to gaze out her side window as it glided out of view. "I can't wait to tell Trina. This makes the drive worth it."

"You mean worth being stuck in a car with me?"

"I have a question about that." Scarlett took her chance. "Why are you going to Fairbanks instead of catching a plane back to California? I thought you and Carole were leaving today."

"She was planning to, not me. When she said she was staying another day to work, I decided to go ahead with the road trip."

"You left her with Hudson again. It's none of my business, but you're okay with that?" She kept her eyes on the road, afraid her question was too personal.

He ran a hand through his neatly trimmed hair and then across the scruff on his chin.

"You're taking a long time to answer, Doctor."

"Absence makes the heart wonder, doesn't it?" he commented without looking at her.

"Sorry," was her awkward reply. She watched the scenery roll past her window. Why was she pressing him about Carole? Her own wondering was going to be tested in two short days when she saw Alan again. She tried not to think about it, instead honing in on the relief of warmer weather and seeing her family. And sleeping in her own bed. No more chairs or space heaters.

"I apologize, Gil," she blurted out. "I shouldn't have let you drive me all this way when you have your own stuff to worry about. You should be finishing your dad's office."

"Too late. Here's the exit." GPS navigated them to the empty parking lot of the Santa Claus House on St. Nicholas Drive. The sprawling white building decorated in Christmasy snow scenes and charming red accents was definitely closed.

Gil read from a sign on the door. "I don't think Santa's home." His breath came out in puffs.

Scarlett glared. "He's right there." She pointed to the giant fiberglass Santa Claus statue looming over the entire area. "All forty-two feet and nine hundred pounds of him." She packed her tablet in her purse. "I did my homework."

"Don't you even want to see the reindeer?" He pointed to a

fenced area adjoining the building. "Dasher and Blitzen according to the sign." Indeed, there were two reindeer-looking creatures staring at them.

"Glenda lives in one of the houses down this way," she said, ignoring his attempts to tease her. She wrapped her scarf around her neck a few more times then began the trek across the lot. A knot in her stomach rose to her chest making it difficult to breathe.

"Do you expect me to leave you here?" Gil called from behind.

"I'll be fine. Do what you need to do in Fairbanks, and text me when you're on your way."

"No, I can't do that. I think you need backup."

"Then hurry." She took a deep breath, and the late afternoon cold sliced through her lungs. "I'm sorry. I'm a little nervous," she said when he caught up. "I think it's the one with the wood siding."

"Why are you meeting her at home?"

"No idea." She was too chilled to speak more syllables than necessary.

He stuffed his hat into a pocket and gently grasped her coat at the elbow. "Be careful. It looks icy in spots." They had barely stepped on the stone walkway of the barn-style home when the blue door flung open.

"You're late," a male voice called from the shadowy interior.

"Um, hi there," she called back. "I'm Scarlett Ambrose. I had car trouble, and this kind man, um—this is Gil—he drove me, and we got here as fast as we could. All the way from Anchorage. We came, um . . ." She couldn't keep her teeth from chattering, and speaking was next to impossible as they stepped carefully toward the porch. Talking on the phone with Glenda had been challenging. Scarlett wasn't sure she was ready to meet her face to face. At some point Gil's hand had moved from her elbow to her back, and she found herself relaxing slightly into his firm hold.

He must have considered her pause a chance to chime in. "Is Mayor Sprouse here?" he asked.

Scarlett appreciated his remembering the name and getting

straight to the point when she couldn't. He was right about her needing backup.

"Mama!" the voice shouted. "She's here!" Then a guy emerged on the porch wearing a heavy coat, sturdy boots, and a fur-lined hat similar to Gil's.

Gil cleared his throat and nodded almost imperceptibly toward the other guy's head.

"Go for it," she murmured under her breath.

While Gil pulled on his hat, the guy, who appeared to be about their same age, led them to an eclectic circle of rustic wood and wrought iron patio chairs surrounding a makeshift fire pit. She took the seat he offered, her lungs and throat burning from the cold. Was the discussion really going to happen outdoors?

"Bo! Get the marshmallows." That was their introduction to Glenda, a round-faced woman with waist-length, gray hair. She matched her son, except her hat was lined in red-brown fur. She carried a teapot and four sturdy mugs on a tray and thick wool under each arm. At least hot chocolate and blankets appeared part of the deal.

"I'm Scarlett. This is Gil. Thank you so much for inviting me up here. North Pole seems to be a lovely place." Faded block lettering on the side of one of the cups caught her eye: BEST MAYOR EVER. She stifled her reaction, but Gil had noticed too.

"Mugs are not legally binding," he muttered into his shoulder, and she had to work harder to keep a straight face. They small-talked in bits and pieces about the town and the history of Santa Claus House while they waited, apparently for Bo, because once he showed up, cocoa was passed around, and Glenda launched into all the reasons working with Micki Blanding was a bad idea.

Tucked beneath their rough, wool coverings, Scarlett and Gil nodded when appropriate, and sipped hot chocolate when it wasn't. And avoided looking at the woman's mug.

Abruptly, Glenda stopped mid-sentence. "Bo, light the fire. No sense freezing these people to death."

"Oh, thank you," Scarlett sputtered. She was near there already. She set her mug next to the teapot, positioning herself to fill the gap in the woman's narrative while Gil stood to help Bo at the nearby wood pile. "Mayor Sprouse, I appreciate everything you've expressed, but you need to know that I know that North Pole and the Santa Claus House are at the heart of the Christmas spirit of this state. I know about the thousands and thousands of visitors that come every year. I know about the letters to Santa that are received at your post office and about the letters from Santa mailed to children throughout the world. Without your sponsorship, there is no way to promote Alaska's Christmas spirit."

"We do not have a Christmas spirit problem." Glenda repeated her standard line.

"You're right," Scarlett answered, grateful for the progress made on the fire. The conversation needed all the warmth it could get. "This is not about saying Alaska does or does not. It's about highlighting all the best there is at Christmastime." She held up her tablet displaying an image of the entry form that would be distributed throughout the state's interior with North Pole featured across the top. "You're it."

Glenda straightened in her seat. She seemed to be agreeing with at least that much. Gil and Bo sat again, and no one spoke as the fire flickered and sparked and caught hold.

"So what do you do?" Glenda interrupted the fire's trance, obviously directing her question at Gil.

"I'm a primary care doctor. I'll be joining a practice in Los Angeles in January."

"What are you doing here?" Tact not her forte.

Gil explained briefly about his father's death and packing of the office.

"I knew a professor there at the college. Went to high school with him. Bo, get that book." Bo seemed to know exactly what she was talking about because he left the circle and returned holding a cream-colored book with the author's name in Christmas green across the bottom: Gilbert T. Pennington.

Scarlett drew in a quick breath and pressed a gloved hand to her mouth.

"My dad wrote that," Gil said.

Immediate tears started down Glenda's cheeks.

CHAPTER 11
Anchorage: 31°
Los Angeles: 74°

"Your Gilbert's boy?" Glenda sniffled. "Bo, get me a tissue!" He obediently returned with a box, and his mother whooshed out three in quick succession. "Your dad signed my book." She opened it to the title page to reveal a mostly illegible inscription in black marker covering the entire page.

Gil picked out the words *Christmas* and *well*, and recognized his dad's sprawling signature. "Do you love Dickens as much as my dad did?"

"To tell you the truth, I bought it because he wrote it. Then I heard he was teaching at the college, so me and Bo went down. I'm sorry for your loss," she said around tears.

Bo nodded, either to verify their trip to Wasilla or to witness that his mother was sorry. Gil wasn't sure. "Thank you, Glenda. I appreciate that. You too, Bo. So obviously you knew him."

"Since fifth grade." She paused to finally get her sniffling under control. "That's when he moved to town. He had a great family. I met your mom, Marie, once. Beautiful girl inside and out. He brought her to Fairbanks right after they were engaged." Glenda hadn't strung that many complimentary words together during their entire visit.

Gil relaxed into his chair, his gloved fingers clasped loosely in his lap. A surprising lightness settled in his chest as Glenda spoke of his father. The two were friends, and somehow that thought thrilled him. Being close to anyone in his dad's beloved Alaska had that effect.

But the meeting was Scarlett's, not his, and she had been patient. He chose his words carefully. "Do you know why my dad loved Charles Dickens so much? Because Dickens seemed to care about people. He cared about helping the poor and needy. He cared about giving. Right, Scarlett?" He turned toward her, hoping she would take his lead.

"Exactly." She chimed in as perfectly as if they had planned it. "And Santa Claus is all about giving. He's about sharing and spreading Christmas cheer. The Dickens Village will focus on giving too, by collecting donations to help the needy and by bringing joy into the lives of so many this season. North Pole and Charlestown together help create the wonder and magic of Christmas." She held up the tablet again. "Of course, with North Pole getting top billing."

Glenda sat expressionless with an occasional dab of tissue to the corners of her eyes. Gil exchanged a glance with Scarlett while Bo fiddled with the fire. They waited for the mayor to speak when she was ready.

"I'll stand by the original agreement," she said finally.

Gil sensed Scarlett relaxing slightly as she let go of a breath. "Thank you so much," she said.

"Bo, douse the fire." It must have been Glenda's way of saying the meeting was over because she stood, and they all followed suit.

He had more questions, though. "How well did you know my dad?"

"Gilbert was a very good friend, especially in high school. We were part of a tight-knit group that did everything together. He was a sweetheart, even then."

"Do you happen to know someone from Fairbanks by the name of Ves or Vester?"

"Robert." She said it as if the answer was obvious. "He went by Ves. Best buddy of your dad's at Lathrop High."

"Do you happen to have an address for him?" After receiving the information, he and Scarlett said their thank yous and retraced their walk across the parking lot to the rental car. She was quiet so he didn't say anything, not wanting to intrude on her thoughts.

Once inside, she erupted. "What just happened?" She smacked her palms against the dash. "I can't believe it! Who'd have thought she'd have a copy of your dad's book?" She shook her head at him. "Gil. Talk about backup. Thank you for what you said. Thank you for driving me here." Her palms continued a staccato beat. "I can't believe it."

He smiled at her excitement. "You did it. That was a great speech you gave about North Pole being the center of Alaska's Christmas spirit."

"No," she objected. "I'm buying you dinner. I owe you."

"That I'll accept because I'm starving." On Santa Claus Lane they found a diner where they ate and she rehearsed the entire meeting with Glenda. They laughed about Bo, not sure whether to feel sorry for him or appreciate how he catered to his mother. And they laughed hardest at the Best Mayor mug. Afterward they cruised through North Pole searching out all the Christmas-themed street names possible, finding Kris Kringle, Donner, and Blitzen Drives, and snapping obligatory photos. Candy-cane lampposts lit up as they swung onto one last street.

"I give you Mistletoe Drive," Gil declared. "C'mon. I'll take your picture."

Scarlett posed with a wide smile while she pointed up at the street sign.

"Sorry, but it's Mistletoe. You're sending this to Alan, aren't you?"

She puckered her lips as he maneuvered himself to the correct angle. "Hooey," she said over and over as she tried to keep from shivering.

Finally he gave up and knelt on the sidewalk. Through the lens of his phone camera he framed her from the shoulders all the way up to the street sign. Her blushing-red cheeks and nose and the misty quality of night falling took his breath away. Or was it just so blasted cold in this place? He quickly texted the picture to her.

"That won't do." An elderly couple dressed in bright-colored sweaters and matching caps and gloves rounded the corner. The woman continued, "Hand me your phone. Let's do this right."

"Excuse me?" Gil stood up, but wasn't sure whether to comply.

Then the man spoke. "You heard her. Get in the picture. She does this all the time."

CHRISTMAS FUTURE

Scarlett had dropped the pucker. "We're okay, really."

"No, honey. It's fine." The woman tugged on Gil's coat to lead him toward the sign before plucking the phone from his fingers. "Snuggle up, you two."

The man clapped him on the back before moving out of the frame. "There you go. Now give it all you got."

Gil shrugged at Scarlett and then leaned in thinking it was the only way to get rid of the pair, but he froze when he saw Scarlett's face.

"I don't think so," she said, and then louder, "It's getting late. We'd better go."

Gil retrieved his phone and met Scarlett at the car. "Sorry about that," he started, but she waved away his apology.

"Not your fault," she answered too quickly. "Will you drive me to the North Pole Hotel? I have a reservation."

"You're staying the night?"

"It's late. I brought a bag with me just in case I didn't want to drive up and back in one day. Plus I kept you from going to Fairbanks, so just take all the time you need in the morning. I can work from my hotel room."

He scrambled to make sense of what was happening. Despite the apprehension of meeting with the mayor, they'd had what he thought was a good day. They'd conquered North Pole together, and here she was giving him the cold shoulder. Not that he expected anything, but for her to be so abrupt was jarring.

After dropping her off, he completed the short drive to Fairbanks and booked a room at the first hotel he came to. He'd brought nothing, no change of clothes or toiletries. Offering Scarlett a ride was a snap decision. When he found out Cari was staying in Anchorage, and Hudson was the reason, all he wanted was to leave KWIX as quickly as Scarlett had.

He accepted a toothbrush and some toothpaste from the front desk, then retrieved his phone from the car. He hadn't looked at it all day, except for taking pictures, knowing Cari might be burning it up with excuses for her change of plans.

After removing enough clothing to sleep comfortably, he double-checked the heater and settled into bed to flip through his messages. She'd texted a few times. Twice to ask if he was in Fairbanks and what his plans were, and the third to apologize for letting work take all of her time. His sister asked how the office cleanup was going, blaming lack of sleep for not keeping in better touch.

He'd also missed two calls from a London number, probably from the publisher. Another one came from an LA area code that might be related to the medical practice he was joining. The last was a message from the IT tech, Nate, to report that they'd gained entry into his dad's hard drive through an admin account. None of the data appeared shareable except for a few files containing research. The rest was private, course-related items, things like syllabi, grades, and student work.

He slid his phone onto the bedside table and reached for the notepaper where Glenda had written Robert Vester's name and a place to ask for directions. She said Ves lived off-grid, whatever that meant, but anybody at Axel's Auto Parts could get Gil down the right road. He reached for his phone to Google it, wondering how early in the morning off-gridders woke up, then flipped through again. He worried about calling the publisher with news that the manuscript hadn't been found yet.

His finger hovered over his text messages. *I have a question. Got a minute?* It was a text he missed from Scarlett last night. He reviewed the day, rethinking their conversations. She had introduced him to Bo as a kind man. A kind man who had offered her a ride. For some reason the description rubbed him the wrong way, but he pushed it from his mind. She asked what to do with his dad's books. *The books, that was it.* He returned the phone to the table. No need to call her. He already answered the question.

❄

"Hello. How's it going, Izzy? Guess where I am." Gil carried his yogurt, boiled egg, and jelly Danish to a quiet corner of the hotel's dining area so he could talk.

"At the airport?"

"Not even close. In fact, I think I spoke too soon when I called the publisher." He explained what Nate had said about the contents of Dad's files. "I'm just going to have to look some more."

"But at least you agree that selling it is the way to go. Finally," Izzy said.

"I can feel your eye roll all the way from Spokane."

"Must be the fake eyelashes. Kidding! No time or money for that anymore," she lamented. "So you must not be at Dad's office."

"I'm in Fairbanks." He shared Nate's stories of the fishing trips and the pertinent details of meeting the mayor of North Pole. His hope that Izzy wouldn't ask questions was short-lived.

"Wait. Why were you in the North Pole talking to the mayor?"

He paused to consider her answer. "Gave a ride to someone who had car trouble." It was the truth, and she bought it.

"What a happy coincidence that the mayor knew Dad, and they were even friends. How cool is that?"

"Yeah, that's why I'm calling. Do you remember when Dad died and we received some cards from up here?"

"Sure, yeah. The college sent that bouquet."

"I'm just curious about the cards. I guess I assumed they were all from people he hadn't known that well, but was that it? Were there any from old friends?"

"I still know where they are. Do you want me to look?"

"Can you?"

"Let me put Ember down. Call you back in a few."

Gil finished his continental breakfast, dumped his trash, and then headed to hotel checkout. Traveling light, as in with nothing, had its advantages. There was no suitcase to pack or to lug in and out. After his shower earlier, he felt funny putting his day-old clothes back on, but he was going off-grid today. Surely there clean clothes were not required. He wanted some information, a frame of reference, before finding Ves. When had that last fishing trip taken place? Had he kept in close contact with Dad? Did he know about his death?

After dropping off the key card, Gil sat in his car waiting for the heater to warm up and for Izzy to call. He studied the streets of Fairbanks on his phone, but his thoughts strayed to Scarlett, wondering about her night spent at the North Pole Hotel, wondering about his desire to text or call her to find out. He should have been checking in with his fiancée, not a random stranger, no matter how many times they seemed thrust together. But too early to call Cari.

He put the car into drive and exited the hotel parking lot. Snow had fallen during the night, and a pristine whiteness covered every surface except for the streets where the early snowplows had been. He found Lathrop High School and drove past slowly, regretting that he hadn't asked Glenda Sprouse more questions. He wondered where his dad lived. Where was home for him in Fairbanks? Dad's family wasn't native to Alaska. He had been ten when a job change brought them from Illinois, but his love for the place ran deep. He stayed behind after graduation, even though his parents and younger siblings moved soon after.

He pictured his dad as a teenager, ending school on a Friday afternoon and piling in the car to drive out to his favorite fishing spot with his own dad at the wheel and his younger brothers behind, jostling and kidding each other. Their gear would have been inspected twice over, then loaded, along with foil dinners expertly packed by his mother. At least that had been Gil's own experience when Dad took him and Izzy on the same kinds of outings in Southern California, where they grew up. If Mom came, she relaxed into her most recent book-club selection while Dad patiently baited their hooks and showed them how to cast. Other times Mom stayed home saying, "You go have your time with Dad," and Gil imagined she told his father the same.

Why didn't I come to Alaska to fish? His dad had mentioned it a few times, but it never sank deep enough. It never penetrated his busyness. Because Gil was busy. Nothing mattered to him except go here, be there, help here. He hadn't allowed himself to slow down except for his occasional weekends in LA or the trips to Spokane.

His phone rang. Izzy. "Okay," she began, "cards from Glenda, John, Sandra, and Darlene and the English department, Richard and the IT department, and a Wes and Ruthie. No, Ves, I think. Hard to read the writing on that one."

"Ves, that's it. What does he say?"

"'So long to an old friend. I'll remember him at'—sorry can't tell what it says, but it must be a place—'this summer. May he enjoy those . . . heavenly . . . lakes and streams that are even

CHRISTMAS FUTURE

more blue and clear than the ones we grew up with.' Aww, then he writes this, 'And enjoy reuniting with his dear Marie—his love for her even greater than his love for Alaska.' On the front of the card is someone catching a gigantic fish."

"That's the guy. Thanks, Iz."

Gil stopped at the parts store Glenda had specified and received instructions for finding the dirt road he wanted. It led into a grove of trees behind the shop. After driving for what felt like too many miles and surely must have been the wrong direction, he came upon a small log home. His gaze took in the snow-dusted solar panels to the left and an outsized greenhouse and garden plot to the right before he stepped up to the porch to knock.

The door opened, and a woman said, "Git yourself inside, young man, before you freeze."

He entered, then paused to give his eyes time to adjust. "Hello. I'm looking for Ves?"

A stocky man, with a ruddy face taken over by a thick white beard, stuck out a bear-paw of a hand. "Ves here."

Gil took the offer. "I'm—"

"Nah. Like you mean it." The man gripped tighter.

Gil accepted his hand back before continuing. "I'm Gilbert's son." If he thought the handshake was tight, the explosive hug that followed his announcement was on another level.

"What do you know, Ruthie? Gilly's boy is here in our humble abode."

Soon his dad's Alaska, the one in Gil's imagination, came to life as Ves filled the morning with story upon story of two best friends with a shared love for home, the frozen tundra of the last frontier. Finally, Ruth inserted a question about staying for lunch.

"I really can't. I've got a long drive ahead of me." Gil checked his phone to find a text Scarlett had sent earlier. It was almost noon. She was probably anxious to get on the road.

Don't worry about me. I called an Uber and I'm already on my way to Anchorage. Thanks so much for everything. Enjoy Fairbanks.

The message felt like a punch to the gut. He was a nice

man, no, a kind man, she'd said yesterday. But not so kind that she thought he would drive her back to Anchorage apparently.

"My plans just changed," he said.

Soon they gathered at the butcher-block table to share in the simple meal prep, now with Gil taking the lead in the conversation. "Did you know my dad was an author?"

"Sure, sure," Ves said. "He was working on a book when he moved here. Sometimes he'd come up on weekends with his yellow legal pad and sit on the porch and write. In the summer anyway. Into fall and winter, he was inside by the fire. California ruined him for anything below 45 degrees, so I had to give him a hard time about that. Of course, he was losing weight. Not looking like himself."

Legal pads. Made sense. Gil knew where to look when he was back in the office.

"I always sent him home with a big ol' container of venison stew, just like these leftovers we're eating right now," Ruth said.

"It's really good. Thank you for watching out for him." Gil downed another bite. "What do you know about him agreeing to move away from here when he married my mom?"

"Oh, that? He never told you?" Ves filled his own bowl with seconds. "Marie said let's live in Fairbanks or Anchorage, wherever you can get a teaching job, but it was your dad who said they needed to help her mom because of her dad's Alzheimer's, and Marie loved him for it. You see, as much as he loved Alaska, he loved your mother more."

Gil took a moment to let his last bite find its way past the lump in his throat. How he missed his parents. Now he and Izzy were the next generation, the ones to keep the memories of their love alive. "Sorry to get personal, but if he were here I'd ask him how he knew such a big sacrifice would be worth it?"

"Alaska was a big one. That's for sure." Ves said.

Gil smiled at the pun, but the question still troubled him. He'd been trying to figure out the answer for a long time.

Ruth placed her veined, weathered hand on his across the table. "When being with that person feels like home. Your dad told me that not long before he passed."

Now Gil couldn't swallow, or even talk, due to the emotions that welled up, but Ves broke the silence with his booming voice. "So your dad said you were engaged. Are ya' not hitched yet?"

Gil answered with a quick shake of his head.

"Don't put off what you hafta do, son. If I don't start splitting logs the moment it warms up in the spring, I might not have enough to keep us through winter. No sense jawing about things. You go and do it."

"I think what Ves is trying to say is that your dad just knew. He actually compared it to sledding. Falling in love with Marie was as easy as sitting down at the top of a snow hill and then, swoosh, enjoying the exhilaration of the ride."

Manuscripts written on legal pads and his dad's advice on love. They crisscrossed Gil's thoughts as he retraced the dirt path away from the Vesters' place in the woods. Driving all the way back tonight didn't make sense, so he headed to the same hotel, a little embarrassed at the thought of needing another toothbrush. He'd tossed the one he received last night thinking he would be back in Wasilla. Where his clean clothes were too.

A text from out of town cemented new plans. He called Cari.

"Gil, why aren't you returning Loren Medical's phone calls?" She spoke before he had the chance.

"What?"

"Well, I just happened to be talking to one of the receptionists today, and she said . . ."

Checking up on him, no doubt. "Don't worry about it. I'll go see them when I'm down there."

"You're going home?"

"Home. Well, sort of. That's why I'm calling. Remember Anthony Garcia? He was one of my patients? It's been one year since his mom was declared cancer free. I promised him that I'd come on her one-year anniversary and take them to dinner. I just found out it's tomorrow."

"Which one's Anthony?"

"You know. The one that loves Batman."

"Didn't they all?"

"No. Remember the debate last Christmas over who was better, Batman or Superman?"

"I don't remember, sorry."

"But you remember Anthony. He was my buddy."

"They were all 'your buddy.' How did you tell them apart?"

"Forget it. What I'm trying to say is will you come with me? I promised that no matter where I was or what I was doing, I would be there."

"You're going to fly all the way to LA, then drive hours to Blythe because of a promise to a boy who probably barely remembers you?"

"See, you do remember. But he doesn't live there anymore. He and his mom moved to Tucson."

"Arizona?"

"Cari, it's just the weekend. I'm thinking I'll fly out tomorrow and come back Sunday. I thought you were anxious to get out of here."

"I am. Didn't I tell you I'm freezing?"

"Then Arizona. Perfect."

"But Hudson . . ."

"You know what? I get it," he said, his tone even. "You have Christmas Carole to worry about." He wasn't going to beg. He hung up, his mind crowded with conversations from earlier. His dad just knew, Ruth had said. *Like swoosh.* "No sense jawing about it," Ves said. "Just do it."

After his weekend trip, he would take Cari to a really nice restaurant to break off their engagement. It wouldn't be the beach, but it would be the antithesis of that bench in the desert where he proposed to her.

He pulled up Alaska Air's website on his phone and reserved one seat to Tucson out of Fairbanks International.

CHAPTER 12
Anchorage: 31°
Phoenix: 88°

Scarlett thanked the Uber driver at the curb in front of KWIX, rating him five stars because he had kept the heater going strong all the way from North Pole. He'd been forced to remove his coat to endure it, but he didn't seem to mind. Earlier in the day, Daniel had arranged for a mobile mechanic to replace the battery in the company car, but since her VIP pass was hanging from the rearview mirror, the trick would be getting the vehicle out of the parking structure. She avoided eye contact as she entered then maneuvered toward the north lobby of the building, rolling her small bag behind. If she found the right exit, she might avoid having to speak to anyone.

"Miss Ambrose?"

Her hopes fell when she heard her name called by the studio receptionist. She approached the desk quickly.

"This was left for you earlier today. He said to call if you have any trouble." The woman held out a business card from the mechanic, but Scarlett froze. Carole and Hudson were standing in front of the exit doors locked in an embrace. Maybe *locked* and *embrace* were too strong of a description, but they were huddling. Closely. She had tried to warn Gil about the two of them. Again, not her problem. She'd fought thoughts of Gil on the way to Anchorage, so embarrassed that she had allowed him to drive her all the way to North Pole and that somehow they ended up on Mistletoe Drive. What was she thinking?

She snatched the card, slipped it into her purse, and crossed the lobby. The TV producer had headed down the hall, but she couldn't avoid Carole. Or Cari. Whatever her name was.

"Scarlett." Carole eyed the bag on wheels. "Are you coming or going?"

"Actually, I just got back. I'm picking up my car." Scarlett didn't stop. Maybe Carole would take the hint.

"I'm leaving too. Let's walk out together."

Carole's phone chortled, but she seemed determined to keep stride even while taking the call. "Of course, this is Tiffany." She laughed. "No, not a problem. I'll fly out this weekend. I am so done here." She ended the call and immediately addressed Scarlett again. "So did you get what you needed from Gil, I mean, the information you wanted for your little Christmas show?"

Scarlett took a breath before answering, her gaze lingering on her car. She was that close to getting away. "I'm good. How about you? How is your—" she swallowed the word *little*— "Christmas show here going?"

Carole must have interpreted her hesitation as curiosity. "That call was from my agent. I have a third interview for a jewelry hostess in LA. I'm pretty excited."

Scarlett raised her eyebrows. "Does KWIX know about this?"

Carole waved her manicured fingers. "This is how the game is played. You keep your options open. I'm sure it's the same with marketing or whatever it is you do. You know."

Actually I don't know. Is it the same with men? Scarlett wanted to ask. She hit the button to unlock her car, prepared to end the conversation before she said the wrong thing. "Let me know how it works out for you."

"I land about 4:30. What time do I need to be ready for the dinner?" Scarlett slipped on a pair of comfortable shoes, and tossed underwear into a large tote. She could travel light since she'd left plenty of T-shirts and shorts back in Arizona.

"Aren't I picking you up from the airport?"

"My mom wants to." She added toiletries to a small pile

next to her bag, ignoring Alan's attempt to interrupt. "She knows we'll spend the entire weekend together, and she'll hardly see me. She asked for this one concession."

His silence meant he would go along with it, but not without sarcasm. "Why not? It's only been three months since I've seen my fiancée. I don't need to greet her at the airport. You know, if you're in the area, just drop by and say hi, if you have time."

"Alan. We have the dinner, we have all day tomorrow, and then I thought we could go trick-or-treating with my nieces. Just tell me what time to be ready tonight."

He was quiet again. Then he said, "I'll pick you up at 7:00."

"I'll be ready."

"I'm more than ready." He sounded like the real Alan again. "Can't wait to see you, babe."

"Me too. I really have to go, though. If I don't finish packing, I'm not going anywhere."

"I love you, Scar. See you tonight."

"Love you."

Thirty minutes later she slid her travel bag into the back seat of the Uber and followed it in.

"Going to the airport, right?" the driver asked.

"South terminal, please. Flying Delta. I'm actually going somewhere much warmer."

"Good for you."

After passing through security at the airport, she found a seat near her gate and brought up Trina's name on her phone. She'd wanted to talk to her ever since Heath asked about planning an engagement party, but the call went to voicemail. "Hey, Trina. It's Scarlett. I'm off to Arizona, but we need to talk. Don't make any crazy plans with Heath. Well, that's not what I mean. Just keep an open mind and we'll talk when I get back." She wished she had discussed the subject with Gil, but he hadn't responded to her text, and then she had forgotten all about it.

❄

Warmer.

Everything about being back in Arizona was warmer. The

T-shirt weather. Meeting both her parents at the airport because her dad had taken off work a little early. Even getting lost in Alan's enthusiastic embrace when he picked her up for dinner. She had been too busy to realize how much she missed all these things. Except for the weather. She definitely remembered how much she missed that. The temperature in Alaska had been in her face and chilling her to the bone every day since summer ended. But Alan? Maybe absence did make the heart grow fonder.

After the awards were presented at the dinner event, one of the managing partners announced that Alan had made junior at the law firm. During dessert Alan leaned in close to her ear. "Babe, I have another surprise. My parents are taking us to Hawaii for Thanksgiving, all my sisters and their husbands and kids. What do you think about you and me on the beach at a turkey luau?"

She stuck a fork in her cherry cheesecake. "Hawaii? For Thanksgiving?" Her thoughts immediately flew to Alaska and her Christmas spirit project, plus opening day at the Dickens Village had yet to be determined.

"We fly out Wednesday, come back Monday."

She pulled back to look at him, hating that she didn't feel excited about it. "You didn't think to ask if that schedule would work for me?" This was the same guy who wanted her opinion on every last detail of his marriage proposal. Gil would have to weigh in on this. Except she'd decided she was done blowing up his phone with her relationship what-ifs.

Alan straightened in his seat to accept congratulations from an elderly couple passing by their table, then leaned in again. "You said you'd be home by Thanksgiving. I wanted to surprise you."

She raised her eyebrows and smiled through a bite of cheesecake. First Heath and now Alan. What was it with surprise trips to Hawaii?

He took her free hand in his and gently caressed it, his voice softening with his touch. "You've been colder than anyone deserves to be, Scarlett. I thought what's the best thing for you but Hawaii?"

He thought he knew what was best for her, but he was seeing only a few pieces of the puzzle. She filled her mouth with cheesecake instead of with what she wanted to say. Something like maybe absence didn't make the heart grow fonder. Alaska had frozen not only her toes and the tip of her nose, but her heart. Barely in town a few hours and here she was wondering.

Alan tightened his grip and placed his mouth against her ear. "I love you, babe. I'll do whatever you want." He kissed her before pulling back slightly. "I'll tell my mom you can't make Hawaii. I'm sure she can get a credit for the ticket."

"Thank you." She allowed herself to melt a little into his gaze. With his broad shoulders fitted nicely into his tasteful dark suit he was looking every bit a partner in a prestigious law firm. She squeezed his hand. "Hey, why don't you come up and have Thanksgiving with me and be there for my opening day?"

He let go of her hand and moved to arm's length. "I can't miss Hawaii with my family, Scarlett. We're not married yet, so my mom will let you off the hook, but not me. And not you once we're married, by the way. She has to have everyone there. You know that's her thing."

What about my thing? She shook the thought away. She couldn't expect him to give up his plans if she wasn't willing to give up hers. But her reasons were work-related.

Several guys in nice suits of varying conservative hues, interrupted, crowding around Alan to pat him on the back and talk about what lawyers talk about. When they dispersed, he said, "I see one of my old law professors. I'll be right back."

Scarlett pulled out her phone. Apparently the Hawaii trip was case-closed. While finishing dessert, she answered texts from her mom and sister, then brought up the picture Gil had sent of her on Mistletoe Drive. She almost shivered remembering the crisp, cold air and the contrast between all her layers and the sweaters the elderly couple wore as they bopped down the street.

Don't worry about me. I called an Uber. She cringed a bit at her last message to him. She hoped it sounded light and breezy, not rude. She just needed some distance between them. He was funny and kind, a perfect gentleman. And looked better than anybody in a T-shirt or a silly beaver hat. But he was engaged. *For better or for worse*, she thought wryly, when an image of Carole and Hudson in the KWIX lobby flashed in her memory.

She watched Alan across the room talking it up with anyone

who came by to commend him for his achievement award and for making junior. He didn't seem to care that he was going to Hawaii without her. She had hoped to be home by Thanksgiving, but she had made it clear it was only a guess. She had to see the projects through to the end. He should understand that. Maybe she was engaged for better or for worse too.

But she wouldn't settle for worse, and it wasn't fair to Alan to continue their relationship if she had doubts. And couldn't stop thinking about a certain doctor she met in Alaska.

She began a text to Gil. They had discussed engagements at length. Why not how to break them off? A text from him popped up before she could finish. *Sorry, I didn't respond the other night. Thought I would check to see if you still had a question.*

She had wanted his opinion about Heath. She deleted what she wrote and started over.

Scarlett: *So you know Trina that's engaged to Heath?*

Gil: *The fish guy?*

Scarlett: *The fish guy. He wants to have a surprise engagement party.*

Gil: *But she knows they're engaged, doesn't she?*

Scarlett: *That's not the surprise. He wants to have a party and surprise her with a trip to Hawaii where they will get married on the beach.*

Gil: *And she's not going to love it?*

Scarlett: *She wants a church wedding in the same church her grandfather preached at. I tried to explain it to Heath but he's only focused on Hawaii.*

Scarlett: *He's been given two tickets to the destination of his choice. A bonus from work, I think.*

Scarlett: *Just like a guy. Only looking at one part of the puzzle.*

Scarlett: *Ignore that first sentence*

Gil: *Ignoring*

Gil: *Sorry, they brought more tacos.*

Scarlett: *And I'm just having prime rib. Pace yourself.*

Gil: *I'm really proud of Heath for getting employee of the month at the fish store for 12 months straight.*

Scarlett: *I'm serious. What do I do?*

Gil: *Keep explaining until he gets it.*

CHRISTMAS FUTURE

Alan suddenly caressed her shoulders and leaned down to kiss her neck. "I've had enough. Are you ready to go, babe?"

She quickly palmed her phone into her purse and stood to cross the room with him to the lobby.

As they waited for the valet to bring the car around, he pulled her close. "Maybe you can fly to Hawaii after your grand opening. I'll stay an extra couple days, and we'll have some time for just us. I've missed you so much." His lips found hers, lingering until a guy appeared with keys.

Alan led Scarlett to the open car door, then climbed in the driver's side. "I went to dinner with T.J. and Lexi a couple of weeks ago, and they were giving me such a hard time about it, but it's true. I hate being apart, Scarlett." He reached for her hand while merging into traffic.

She snapped it away. "Excuse me? Dinner with T.J. and Lexi? Are you serious?"

"I know how you feel about Lexi, but—"

"It's obvious you don't, Alan."

"You gotta let it go, Scar. They paid back your money. It's been almost a year."

"It's been ten months and one week, and I know I'm the only one counting, but you know it's not about the money."

"You can get past this. What about Ambrose and Bloom? Your dream?"

"Did you ask her about that? At dinner?"

"Don't give up everything, Scarlett. You have to think about the future. What you want."

She wanted out of the car. She wanted to not be having this conversation.

"Congratulations on your success, Alan," she said, her jaw tight. "Will you drop me off at my sister's? She's sick, and her husband's at work. She's letting the girls stay up late to watch a movie, but they're probably going to be crazy. I told her I'd come help get them to bed."

"Good practice." He smiled.

"Yeah, wanna come?" She felt particularly combative. She knew he wouldn't.

"Oh, babe. My parents are expecting me by ten to celebrate making partner. Didn't I tell you?"

No big deal if he'd rather be with his parents. He already proved that.

Later, after snuggles and Halloween bedtime stories, Scarlett watched her favorite, tender little redheads drift off to sleep. Soon her own eyes drooped as she fluffed a pillow and reclined next to three-year-old Maci. Scarlett had been up too early and on a plane or sitting in airports all day. Travel fatigue weighed on every part of her body. Her nieces cooed and sighed in their sleep, a sweet lullaby to her ears. She wanted this in her future. Someday. Whether in a warm place or cold, family was what mattered.

Wasn't that Alan's point about Hawaii, though? Family? The question jarred her awake for a moment, and then she let it go. Somehow it felt different than when Gil talked about his family. She smoothed down Maci's wispy curls and pulled up the sheet that had been kicked off. She wanted this, but it had to be with the right person.

She lifted her phone to send a text, shielding the light from the two sleeping beauties.

I'm here in Phoenix for the weekend. Wondering what your thoughts are about breaking off engagements—preplanned or no?

CHAPTER 13
Los Angeles: 80°
Anchorage: 28°

Gil spent Saturday morning on the phone tying up loose ends as much as possible for a non-work day. Fortunately in October Anchorage was only one time zone away from Arizona. He left a message for Darlene about his dad's desktop computer. Nate had emailed the research files, but the rest of the data was school property. Gil added an apology for needing more time to finish clearing out the office, but he'd get back to the college Tuesday and be done with it.

Since leaving Fairbanks, Gil had reflected on Ves's words. The Loren Medical team wanted him. No need to wait until January to join them. In the words of off-gridder Robert Vester, "No sense jawing about it. Just do it" He called the LA office and left a voicemail, letting them know he'd be in town Monday. He'd make that stop before heading back to Alaska.

"Don't put off . . ." He mulled over feasible responses to Scarlett's text—the one he hadn't answered yet. It had been there when he woke up. *What are your thoughts about breaking off engagements?*

And how surprising that she was in Arizona too.

He should keep it light, like their previous texting banter. He couldn't say that he'd been considering the same question, wondering how to break things off with Cari.

He stopped and started his response. *Preplanned or no?* she'd asked. He deleted and started again. *If it's from the heart anything goes.*

103

Then in an effort to add some humor, he dropped a second. *Do you need backup? I'm in AZ.*
 Scarlett: *You mean AK?*
 Gil: *Haha, no. AZ. Really.*
 Scarlett: *???*
 Gil: *Came to celebrate with a former patient. I told him if his mom stayed in remission for one year I'd fly down and take them to dinner.*
 Gil: *Actually I told him when, not if.*
 Scarlett: *You flew all the way to AZ to take a little boy to dinner* ♥♥♥
 Scarlett: *Did you finish your dad's office?*
 Gil: *No*
 Scarlett: *I thought you practiced in California*
 Gil: *They moved to Tucson, so I haven't seen them since last year. And it was more than dinner. It was a full-on fiesta with family and friends and the best tacos I ever had.*
 Gil: ♥♥♥
 Gil: *And yes, that's the first time I've sent hearts in a text. But tacos.*
 Gil: *And can't forget the tamales.*
 Scarlett: 👍

He flipped from messages to phone and hit contacts. He didn't know the time in London, but not surprisingly, the call went to voicemail. "Hey, this is Gil Pennington returning your call. I've had a minor issue with my dad's manuscript, but I'll get it worked out next week and call you then. Thanks for your patience. Talk to you soon."

Minor as in he had a good lead, but he personally was a thousand miles away.

Gil pulled the tag off a new pair of jeans. Unexpectedly traveling light to Fairbanks meant a late-night Walmart run to prep for his early flight out yesterday. Of course, shopping for Arizona weather in Alaska forced him to get creative. He bypassed the long johns and lined flannel button-downs and ended up with a few long-sleeved Tees, some boxers and jeans, and a suitcase to carry them in. He bought a pair of tennis shoes and hoped they would get him through the weekend. Not wanting to leave his thick coat, gloves, and beaver hat behind at the hotel, he had to make room for them as well. Airport security in Phoenix probably enjoyed those items rolling through the conveyor.

He texted Izzy, this time telling her he was in Arizona. Since that would raise questions, he texted again to tell her about Anthony and about how he had a lead on the manuscript and would call next week. He hadn't talked to Cari since their conversation on Thursday, when she said no to coming with him. "Don't put off—" Ves's words again. But ending their engagement over the phone wasn't a good idea. It would have to wait until next week.

He hopped in the shower then dressed to meet the Garcias for an early lunch. He found Eegee's with the help of GPS and caught up to them as they were entering the restaurant. It had been Anthony's choice, so Gil followed the boy's lead when ordering a sub, fries, and the frozen fruit drink the place was known for.

Blanca greeted him as warmly as she had last night. He'd been overwhelmed at the large crowd gathered at the rented hall, when he'd been expecting to treat them to a quiet dinner somewhere. But he shouldn't have been surprised at all the people, the endless food, and the lively music that lasted until almost midnight. Everyone wanted to be a part of celebrating Blanca's good health. Some had even driven from California and New Mexico, and they were all so welcoming, especially when they realized he was Anthony's doctor through his three hospital stays. In fact once he was introduced, they immediately knew who he was. Complete strangers were patting him on the back, asking if his fiancée was with him and offering condolences on his father's death. And they kept filling his plate as if it was his last meal. The best part, though, was seeing six-year-old Anthony's permanent grin.

Sitting across the booth, he wore the same grin watching Gil try his mango eegee's for the first time. "What do you think, Dr. P?"

Gil savored his first bites of the sweet, icy treat. "I think I know why you've been so healthy and happy since moving to Tucson," he quipped.

"You know it," Anthony replied. He dug into his own cup.

Blanca placed her hand on Gil's arm across the table. Her smile rivaled her son's. "And he's especially happy because you're here." Her tone softened. "There was so much going on last night, all the noise and the people, I didn't properly thank you for coming on such short notice. Everything was a whirlwind with preparations and figuring out where to put family. It wasn't until Anthony said, 'What about Dr. P? He said he would come.' I told him not to get his hopes up, but here you are. So thank you." Her smile had changed to grateful tears that she dabbed at with a napkin.

Gil squeezed her hand. "I wouldn't miss it." He winked at Anthony. "Or the eegee's."

"You should have brought your girlfriend. Remember when she gave us all those presents at the Christmas party?" Anthony said through a mouthful of fries before adding a scoop of his strawberry slush to the mix.

"*Mi hijo*, slow down," Blanca scolded.

"She had work to do in Anchorage," Gil replied. It was the easy answer.

Blanca's brow creased with confusion. "Anchorage? Gil, did you fly here all the way from Alaska? When I called you, I assumed you were in California. Just like you to be so selfless."

"Don't start that." He waved a hand at her. "I'm here because I made a promise that no matter where I was . . . wait, no. I'm here because I want to be here. You're family."

She nudged her son's shoulder. "Pay attention, Anthony. You grow up to be a man just like your Dr. P."

Gil stuck his tongue out at Anthony and winked again, and they all laughed.

"Hey, Mama. Can we invite him to our party today?"

"Why not?"

"We're having a Halloween party at the cancer center. You have to come. Please?" Anthony begged.

"We try to do events every now and then at the center in town. I don't want Anthony to forget how blessed we are, you know? Or me either," Blanca said. "You really should come. You're so great with kids. They'll love you."

Gil was on board immediately. He had no plans past lunch, and his flight to LA wasn't until morning. Blanca excitedly began discussing details of the party and even gave him a few assignments since they'd had some help fall through.

"Your girlfriend should have come with presents," Anthony inserted when his mom paused to take a breath.

"*Mi hijo!*" she exclaimed, shaking her head.

They separated soon after with plans to meet early at the center. Back in Gil's hotel room curiosity got the better of him, so he pulled out his phone to see if Scarlett had texted again. Her question about breaking off engagements had devolved into hearts and tacos, and she hadn't even commented on his joke about being her backup. No new texts, but without much thought he started one to her.

Going to have to back out of being backup. Looks like I have a Halloween party at the cancer center to go to. I'm in charge of balloons.

CHAPTER 14
Phoenix: 77°
Anchorage: 28°

Don't do anything rash in the heat of Arizona. That's what Scarlett had told herself as she hiked Camelback that morning, her thoughts full of Alan and what happened last night. With every step planted on the Cholla trail, she relived his choosing Hawaii with his mother, envisioned him sitting down to dinner with Lexi and her husband, and wondered at his avoidance of anything involving children. Even with her nieces.

At the top of the mountain she took a selfie to send to Trina with the caption: *See I really did hike Saturday like I promised. Only a week late!*

She pictured Trina, bundled to the hilt to face the frigid air as she hiked, while Scarlett was feeling warm in a T-shirt and shorts. She'd slept in, so she missed the thrill of sunrise and the accompanying cooler temperature. Some energetic hikers had dressed in costume to celebrate the day, but she didn't envy the Winnie the Pooh and Tigger-too clothed in top-to-bottom fleece. She guessed her mountain view couldn't match Trina's, though. She remembered the drive to North Pole, the stately trees and snow-capped mountains. The eagle's flight against a white sky. When she finally took the time to see, Alaska was startling in its beauty.

Back at her car after finishing the hike, she found her friend's response. A matching hike selfie with the view Scarlett had imagined. Then she reread Gil's reply to her late-night text: *If it's from the heart* . . . But her heart was unsettled. Maybe she needed another trek up the mountain and back to clear her head. It was unsettled too.

Instead she climbed into her reliable Honda, grateful that her parents had let her keep it at the house while she was away. She smiled as she read through her entire texting conversation with Gil, then dropped her phone in her lap and face-planted on the steering wheel. Something was seriously wrong if she'd rather text with a guy she just met instead of text or talk to her fiancé. He had tried both this morning, but she hadn't responded.

But Gil was . . . Gil. What was this pull he had on her? She straightened up in the seat, pulled out her hair tie and redid her ponytail. Just as quickly she was back to her phone. So funny that when she asked about breaking off engagements he'd offered to be backup, and then later texted a retraction. He had flown all the way to Arizona for a little boy and was helping at a Halloween party. That actually sounded more appealing then facing Alan today.

She rolled down both front windows to encourage air to flow through. *Don't do anything rash*, she told herself again. Maybe Alan would understand her need for time and space. She let out a resigned sigh as she imagined his response, *I've given you time since last July. I've given you space all the way to Alaska.* But Alaska was her choice, not his to give.

Last Christmas . . . She couldn't stop the vision dancing through her head of Jared's mumbled singing of that song in Daniel's office last week. But last Christmas, actually Christmas Eve, she had felt good about saying yes to Alan. They'd dated through almost two years of college. It was meant to be, wasn't it? Then what's-her-name dropped the bank account bomb on Ambrose and Bloom Events. Was that when "meant to be" began falling apart? She couldn't help wondering.

She had been blindsided and shell-shocked. She quit her job at the wedding superstore because she wanted nothing to do with Lexi. Her subsequent position at the print shop, though full-time, didn't increase her savings much. With each week and month she grew more and more restless, so that by the time Royce mentioned an internship in faraway Alaska, nothing could keep her from hopping on a plane. Not even a fiancé begging her not to go, though she secretly knew he had to be relieved. Her restlessness affected everyone around her despite her efforts. Actually she hadn't tried hard enough to hide her feelings, kind of like with her job in Anchorage. Everyone knew how she felt about it.

Her phone lit up with her ringtone. Alan. She chugged the last of her water and decided she should answer this time.

"Where are you?" he said. "I went by your house to pick you up for breakfast, and your mom said you stayed at your sister's, but when I called over there, you had already left. And you haven't answered any of my calls."

"I went for a hike."

"Did you go up Piestewa Peak without me?"

"Camelback." She knew he preferred the other hike. It was one they had often taken together.

"I've been thinking about last night. I'm sorry for whatever I said that made you mad."

Scarlett swallowed hard. That was her favorite kind of confession, the kind where he had no idea what he'd said but a blanket apology would cover it. *Right.*

"I have a surprise, but just listen before you say anything. T.J. and Lexi are meeting us for dinner. I know, I know, Scarlett, just listen." He attempted to waylay her indignant interruption.

"Oh, I'm listening. This should be good," she replied as evenly as she could manage.

"I think it's exactly what you need, Scar. Ever since the problem with Lexi you haven't been happy. You haven't been yourself. You need to be face to face and sort it out."

"That sounds like a delightful plan. Did you reserve a table ringside at Jabz?" On a whim she and her sister had spent one summer working out there before abandoning their newly acquired boxing gloves.

"You're not listening to reason."

"I know all about how holding a grudge only hurts yourself. How forgiveness isn't for the other person, it's for you. My mom has done her due diligence, believe me. I also know it can only happen when, I mean if, I'm ready. I don't need to be forced into sitting across the table from her."

Alan sighed into the phone. "I already made reservations at Van Gogh's for the four of us."

CHRISTMAS FUTURE

She let out a breath too. He was going all out for this proposed reconciliation. But she had another idea germinating, and it involved helping blow up balloons for a party just two short hours away from where she was in Phoenix. "Change it to three, Alan. I have an event to attend." She might not have Christmas spirit, but she could muster some for Halloween.

After a quick shower, she hopped onto the freeway, her pulse humming with adrenaline. Apparently her plan was to drive first, figure out details later. As she struggled to keep her speed within the limit, she alternated between berating herself for being the worst fiancée ever in the history of fiancées to applauding herself for taking a stand. And then there was the voice that said she needed to be in Tucson right now at a Halloween party for cancer patients and, in the next moment, what in the world was she thinking? How would she find him? What exactly was going to be her explanation when she arrived, anyway? This was as crazy as flying off to the last frontier of Alaska.

Tucson. Halloween party. Cancer center. Kids. Tucson. Party. Balloons. Her brain was overloading. She called her sister because her mom would ask questions. "Hey, who do we know in Tucson?"

"Bailey Cruz just moved there with her husband."

"Bailey got married? When did that happen?" The Cruzes were their longtime neighbors from down the street, and Bailey was several years younger than Scarlett.

"She legit just met a guy like six weeks ago, and they got married that quick. He actually seemed really nice, and he has a great job. She transferred to the hospital down there. Sorry no one told you."

"No worries, but how might I find her?"

"I'll text you her new number. I helped with flowers for the wedding. They were kind of desperate with it being so quick."

"That is desperate."

"Ha, ha. Are you going to tell me why you're so interested in Tucson?"

"I called you because I knew you wouldn't ask questions like Mom."

"Just tell me if you'll be back in time for trick-or-treating."

"I really did want to, but it's not looking likely. Is that okay?"

"It's fine. I haven't even told the girls it was a possibility since I knew you'd be spending every waking moment with Alan. So you two are off to Tucson on some adventure?"

"Remember what I said about asking questions?"

"Mmm hmm." Her sister's nonverbal reply conveyed her suspicion, but she didn't pry.

"One last thing. What was the name of that library book that Brenna and Maci liked so much last night, the one about the ghost?"

"You mean *Sammy the Not So Friendly Ghost*?"

"That's it. Thanks, Sis. You sound like you're feeling better. Love you."

Scarlett pulled off at the next exit for gas and a Powerade. The car needed fuel, she needed fuel. Really she needed a reason for this adventure, as her sister had called it. She formulated a makeshift plan on the fly as she waited at the pump. First thing was calling Bailey. She found the number her sister sent, but there was no answer on the first or second attempts. Texting would have to do.

Scarlett: *Hey, Bailey! This is Scarlett. I heard you got married. Congrats! I'm in AZ. Wanna meet for tacos?*

Bailey: *Ack! I'm at work.*

Scarlett: *Your hospital has a cafeteria*

Bailey: *Yeah, but…*

Scarlett: *C'mon. Cafeteria tacos. That's a thing, right?*

Bailey: *'Fraid not*

Scarlett: *Just say yes. I need a reason to go to Tucson.*

Bailey: *???*

Bailey: *Where's Alan?*

Bailey: *Okay. Yes. If you tell me what's up.*

Scarlett: *Nothing's up except Halloween. Can you help me with a costume? And point me to the local cancer center?*

Bailey: *I have to go, but I'm at Banner on Campbell Avenue, and so is the cancer center. Text me when you get here.*

Scarlett let out a breath. This was happening.

After arriving in Tucson, she followed GPS to a local bookstore where she looped shopping baskets on both arms to

CHRISTMAS FUTURE

fill with copies of *Sammy* and every other Halloween storybook and activity and puzzle book that caught her eye. She imagined the employees silently cheering her on with each basketful she brought to the counter before going back to fill another as if she was on one of those shopping game shows. It was Halloween Day. They had to be excited to be moving so much stock before it all went to clearance tomorrow. She could only guess how many kids would be at the event, but she didn't care. She was going into that party prepared.

After two employees helped her load her car, she found directions to the hospital where Bailey worked. As she drove, she replayed her plan. She'd grab a few items to create a costume, then deliver the books, maybe pass out some candy. Except she didn't have candy. She tightened her grip on the steering wheel as she kept her eyes pealed for a grocery store, then just as quickly changed her mind. A Halloween party would already have lots of it.

Her thoughts whirled. She'd drop off her trunk load, pass out candy or whatever there was, and maybe even be back to trick-or-treat with her nieces. And in addition to the books, she had a story. She was in Tucson to meet an old friend. *Oh, and, Gil, I just happen to have gifts for the kids.*

Scarlett looked over at the bag she'd placed in her front seat. She was going to Tucson to party with young cancer patients, and they were going to love the books. She flipped the visor down to check her makeup in the mirror, then ran her fingers through her messy beach waves. She hadn't taken much time on her hair after her shower. She should have plucked her eyebrows. She rolled her eyes. *Keep telling yourself it's for the kids.* Was she like Carole last Christmas, breezing in to bring piles of gifts to Gil's patients? A looming red light startled her, and she braked too hard. The car behind her honked. Scarlett sank against her seat and took a deep breath.

Carole. Was she here in Arizona with Gil? He hadn't said as much, but parties and gifts seemed to be her thing. Scarlett eyed the books again, wishing now she had stopped for candy. As in the big assorted packs of full-size candy bars. She shook her head and accelerated responsibly on green. She was not competing with Gil's fiancée on any level. Except if Carole was at the party, Scarlett suddenly didn't want to be. New plan, drop off and go home. No costumes, no anything. Or turn right around and return the books for a refund.

Her ringtone jangled. "Hey, it's Bailey. I'm on break now. Are you close? Are you thinking something medical for a costume?" Maybe if Bailey came with her to the party it would legitimize her reason, Carole or no Carole.

Soon Scarlett arrived at the hospital, and Bailey was supplying scrubs and a stethoscope for a doctor's costume. "Do you want some fake blood? Scaaaaars, maybe?" Her eyebrows moved up and down on repeat.

Scarlett groaned. "Nah, this is for kids. Do you have a clown nose?"

Bailey grunted. "Some people think clowns are scary. You could be bruised and bloodied and have a fake hatchet sunk into your forehead and somehow that's more acceptable. A guy showed up in the ER with a pocket knife in his head last week." She shuddered. "No, thank you."

Scarlett slipped a green surgeon's cap over her hair. "Yeah, I'd like my head intact. Wait. What's that?" She pointed to something furry on a shelf next to boxes of sterile gloves.

"A beaver hat, I think it's called. You might know, your sister said you were working in Alaska. A patient left it behind. A friend had given it to him, and there was some kind of inside joke about it."

"Can I borrow it?" She replaced the green cap with the furry look-alike to Gil's, then pulled on a pair of the gloves. Her heart thumped a little harder in her chest as Bailey gave her directions to the activity room in the oncology wing before heading back to her shift. She was going to see Gil, in Arizona, on purpose. This was getting real.

"Scarlett?" Gil stopped on his way down the hall.

"Hey, Dr. Pennington. Your text sounded like you needed an event planner, so here I am."

CHAPTER 15
Los Angeles: 80°
Anchorage: 26°

"Who's calling who doctor?" Gil laughed and he could feel his smile threatening to take over his whole face. He attempted a more serious tone. "And where did you get that 'silly' hat?"

She splayed her fingers along each side of it in a pose. "You like it? I know where you can get one."

He laughed again, and his heart warmed at the sight of her. He didn't know how to respond. "What are you—? How did you find—?" He stumbled over his words.

"I have an old friend that lives in Tucson now, and I haven't seen her since she got married." Scarlett paused as if searching for words too. "She works here at the hospital, so I thought why not come see if I can help? Surely
doctors know nothing about planning parties."

He scrambled to reply while still trying to makes sense of her explanation. "Do you know anything about costumes? Because I need to be Batman."

"I have no idea how to make that happen, but I can give it a shot. First, do you think there's a dolly somewhere? I've got a bunch of books in my car."

Soon they were side by side wheeling bags down to the activity room. He couldn't stop himself from looking at her every other second.

"Why are you looking at me that way?"

"I can't believe you're here. We were just in Alaska, and now we're both in Arizona. It's just surprising."

"I didn't even decide to come until Wednesday. Alan had an awards dinner. It was kind of a big deal."

Gil perked up at the mention of her fiancé, but he couldn't read anything in her face, and he wasn't going to ask if Alan still retained the title. "And the weekend forecast for Anchorage didn't have anything to do with it?"

"Maybe. What about you. You didn't say anything about going to Arizona either when you were stuck with me in a car for six hours on Thursday."

"Last minute for me too."

A question seemed to cross Scarlett's face then. "Um, did Carole come?"

"No. She couldn't." Wouldn't.

"I just remember you said how much she loved the kids last Christmas. The gifts, the stuffed animals . . ."

"She's really into the Christmas Carole thing right now, so she couldn't leave."

Confusion registered on her face. What was she not saying? "Yeah," she replied finally. "I can relate to that. As much as I complain about my Christmas project, I do want to get it right."

They stacked the books in a corner of the room that was strewn with crepe paper streamers and balloons. "Nice," Scarlett complimented, but her look belied her words.

"Hey, I can tape things to walls and blow up balloons fairly well," he said.

"You got skills." She widened her eyes at him, and her look made him smile. He wanted to continue the conversation, but they were interrupted by a certain enthusiastic six-year-old.

"Dr. P, come meet Miss Jan with me. She's going to play the uk-u-lele." He struggled to pronounce the word. "And sing Halloween songs."

"Anthony, first meet Miss Scarlett. She came down from Alaska too."

"Is this your new girlfriend?"

"No. She just wanted to bring the kids some books."

Anthony gaped at all the full bags. "You carried these all the way from Alaska? That's a lot."

Scarlett held out her hand. "It's nice to meet you, Anthony. And I actually bought the books here. Much easier that way."

He spied one in a bag on top. "*Sammy the Not So Friendly Ghost*? I love that book. My teacher read it to us at school."

"I just read it for the first time last night, and I was like, the kids have to have this."

"Will you read it at the party? Can she, Dr P?"

"Well, I can. I don't know. Is it okay?" Scarlett looked from Anthony to Gil.

"Good idea." Gil ruffled Anthony's hair as Blanca approached with a box of decorations.

"Mama! This is Miss Scarlett. She came down from Alaska with Dr. P, and she's going to read the book I was telling you about."

"Dr. Pennington, you didn't tell us you brought a guest to our Halloween gala."

"I, uh—" he stammered.

Scarlett filled the gap. "I heard you had quite the gala last night."

Blanca put a hand to her heart. "They made a big fuss." She leaned in to Scarlett for a quick embrace. "I'm Blanca."

Scarlett seemed caught off guard by the hug, but recovered quickly. "Oh, I'm Scarlett."

If Gil had known she was coming, he would have clued her in as to what to expect.

"Congratulations on being one year cancer free, Blanca. That's a big deal. And it's so great you're putting on this party."

"We've been blessed."

Anthony pulled on Gil's arm. "C'mon, there's Miss Jan."

"I'll be right back." Gil took the little boy's hand, but turned toward Blanca. "By the way, Scarlett's an event planner. You can put her to work."

The older woman winked. "Maybe she can help these decorations." As Gil walked away, he heard Scarlett giving ideas about where to move the food table.

Before long everything was perfect, with the Scarlett-touch, Gil noted, and young patients, their families, and a smattering of doctors and hospital staff soon filled the space. Laughter and grins accompanied the carnival-style games and activities, and the Halloween-inspired refreshments were a hit. And, thanks to Scarlett's last minute ingenuity, he sported gray scrubs with a pair of black athletic shorts over them, and a black-towel cape safety-pinned at his shoulders. She'd drawn a black mask around his eyes, and he knew he looked ridiculous, but the teasing and smiles he endured were worth it.

Finally Blanca gathered everyone in for story time, and Scarlett took center stage with her animated reading. Gil sat cross-legged on the floor next to Anthony and found himself mesmerized not by the story, but by the rhythm of her voice and her easy manner with the children. He laughed as his little friend couldn't hold back spoilers.

"See, it isn't because Sammy isn't friendly. He really does want to go trick-or-treating with his friends, but he is afraid of the dark. Once they figure it out, they find him a really big light to carry, so that he can visit every house and say 'Trick or Treat' and get candy."

Scarlett must have heard him from where she sat because, much to the little boy's delight, she called him up to help with the story. When it ended, Anthony announced, "See, Dr. P? He just needed a light to show the way."

Gil caught Scarlett's gaze and smiled. *Good job*, he mouthed.

Blanca took Scarlett's place at the front of the small stage. "Thank you. Let's give her a hand." After the clapping tapered off, she continued. "Before Miss Jan leads us in some songs, I have something to say. With everything Miss Scarlett could have been doing this afternoon, she chose to be here with you. Plus she transformed this place." More applause. "What I want to say is, be sure to thank the wonderful doctors, nurses, and staff, and everyone else who helps you on your way to getting better. When I was going through chemotherapy, my little Anthony got very sick and had to be in the hospital like you."

She paused to gain control of her emotions. "It meant everything to me to know that he was being taken care of by a good doctor. He became a member of our family because he didn't just take care of his little patient, he lifted all of our spirits. And can you believe that he flew all the way from Alaska to be here? Dr. Pennington, stand up. I made him do this last night, but he can do it again."

Gil stood as applause built around him. He didn't enjoy

CHRISTMAS FUTURE

being singled out, especially not when he was wearing an impromptu Batman costume. He waved at Anthony who had walked back up on stage at the mention of his name and was waving and beaming from beside his mother. Fortunately she then invited applause for all of the other medical personnel present.

Scarlett touched his elbow and leaned in close, bringing a scent of something flowery. "Quite a tribute, Dr. Batman. We won't tell them your weakness."

"Which one would that be?"

"I've seen you thwarted by a wall of desks. Every superhero has their kryptonite, I guess."

"That's Superman. I think mine's those tacos."

"Tacos?"

"They're setting up leftovers from last night right now."

After the fishing pole had caught its last prize, the last *Sammy* book had been squealed over, and all the black, orange, and purple balloons had been claimed for take-back to hospital rooms, Gil and Scarlett joined in with cleanup.

"Anyone who calls you Scrooge hasn't seen you at Halloween," Gil teased. He scraped tape from a windowsill, then began pulling streamers from the nearest corner.

"Halloween is easy. There are no expectations," she replied, combining her efforts with his, but her look seemed to harden slightly.

Maybe he shouldn't have mentioned Scrooge, even in jest. "I don't know about that. Haven't you ever been disappointed by something dropped in your candy bag?" They both tossed wads of crepe paper into the closest trash can.

"Oh, yeah. Jawbreakers, lemonheads, black licorice." She exaggerated a shiver. "And the cheapies, like gum and suckers. And what's up with 'fun size'? I think it's poorly named. I can think of a size much more fun than that." She pulled a covering off a nearby table.

"When a house gave the full-size candy bars—"

"The stuff of legends." She finished his thought, her eyes widening in that cute way of hers. They shared a laugh. "I wasn't going to say anything, but did you see how Miss Jan was giving the treat table a dirty look?" Scarlett rolled the plastic then sent it sailing to the trash.

"She probably passes out apples to trick-or-treaters."

"She's probably allergic to sugar and happiness," Scarlett added with that wide-eyed look again. "I don't think she smiled once the whole time she was singing."

Blanca called from the entrance to the room. "Do you mind if I leave the rest of these activity books at the nurse's station?"

"Sure. Great idea." Gil and Scarlett spoke at the same time.

"Anthony, *ven conmigo*," Blanca said as she gathered a bag and led him out the doorway. Her family had cleaned up all the food and broken down the tables. The staff had returned to work.

Gil knelt next to Scarlett as she collected candy wrappers that had missed their mark. He added several to the trash, noting her nearness and his increasing desire that she stay that way. He wanted to express his appreciation for her help, but the words lodged in his throat at the sight of her. The scent of her.

She moved away to another area of the room to gather cupcake crumbs and scrub frosting spills.

He exhaled and found his voice. "You don't have to do that. They said someone will come in to do the floor later."

"Sorry, force of habit. Part of any perfect event is getting the cleanup right." She moved from kneeling to a sitting position against the wall, and pulled off her hat. "It must be time to return the beaver," she said.

"Before it turns into a pumpkin?" He dropped down next to her. "Scarlett, I can't thank you enough for helping. You were amazing."

He reached out to lengthen a twist of blonde hair that had flattened while under the hat. He wanted to ask how it ended with Alan. How the breakup went. Couldn't they discuss it and dissect it as they had their proposal stories and her coworker's story? She had to be the one to bring it up, though.

His hand froze. She was looking at him. With a look of . . . what, he wasn't sure. He drew back the gesture and adjusted his sitting position, putting them even closer. Too close for normal breathing. Normal conversation. But he tried. "I loved how you had Anthony come up to do the sound effects for that ghost story. His smile was big enough to break his face."

"That wouldn't be good." She reached out to touch the line

where the side of his smile began. "Don't break your face, Gil. It's a nice face."

Yours too, he wanted to say, but the words felt cheesy forming in his mouth. When she said it, it was perfect. His skin warmed beneath her fingertip, even through the sterile glove. She dropped her hand far too soon. He shifted, attempting to control his breathing, but it wasn't working.

"I blame you for making me smile." He cringed at what ended up coming out. It was cheesy enough, but at least she didn't call him on it.

Instead, she leaned forward so he could see only her profile as she took a deep breath. "If we were texting right now, I would ask you this question." She stopped and started again. "Do you think a couple should hold hands before they have their first kiss? Yes? No? It depends on the situation?"

He cupped his hand over hers, and she gently pivoted toward him, a vision in doctor's scrubs. Barely a whisper of a moment passed, and he pressed his lips to hers, softly and tentatively at first, and then with more intention. She seemed to be returning it with the same.

"I'll take that as a yes," she said when they parted.

"And I would text you back and say yes. That's where the fish guy went wrong. He skipped a few steps." He attempted to lighten the mood while getting his breathing under control.

"So this was unexpected." She rotated away from him slightly.

"But not totally unwanted, I hope." He released her hand.

She didn't answer.

"Too soon? I mean I've wanted to kiss you since that lady told us to on Mistletoe, so it feels like forever to me." He laughed so she'd think he was joking. "It's no Mistletoe Lane, but hopefully no spook alley either."

Fortunately she laughed too. He stood and reached out to help her up, making sure to keep her close. "Actually maybe I wanted to kiss you that night we were stuck in my dad's office." *Stop rambling.*

"Before or after I yelled at the furniture movers?"

"Before. After. During."

"You're so weird." She touched his face again.

He squeezed her hand. "I try."

"Gil, I . . . we . . . but . . . I can't finish a sentence."

"I have that effect on people. And I'm weird."

"Well, I've never been kissed by Batman, so this is definitely a first." She freed a hand to tug on his cape.

He refrained from making a comment about recognizing his bat signals. Instead he caught her eyes with a look that he hoped conveyed what he was feeling. "Let me correct what I said earlier. Not you were amazing, but you *are* amazing."

CHAPTER 16
Phoenix: 77°
Anchorage: 28°

"All right, you two. Should we continue this party somewhere else?" Blanca appeared at the door, her eyes blazing.

Scarlett disentangled herself from Gil, her cheeks burning. How long had the woman been standing there? No Anthony in sight, though. Maybe they would avoid his innocent, but brazen questions at least. Like, Dr. P, why are you kissing her if she's not your girlfriend? Gil would be on the spot for that, not her, but she had plenty of her own probing to do. Why had she allowed what just happened to happen? She'd touched his face, talked about holding hands before kissing. What was she thinking? Why was she even here? She mentally facepalmed at the thought that she'd driven a hundred miles to see him. What kind of message did that send?

Blanca continued, "You're welcome to come back to the house for coffee."

Not for more kissing. Scarlett ruefully completed what Blanca must have been thinking.

Gil looked in Scarlett's direction, but she buried herself in her phone. She'd missed multiple calls and texts from Alan. Pangs of guilt rose rapidly from her stomach to her chest, then threatened to lodge in her throat. "I have to go. If I leave now I might get back in time to trick-or-treat with my nieces." Her eyes flashed over the time on her phone. Almost 5:45. With a two hour drive between here and there, the girls would be home sorting out their candy haul by then.

"Plus I have a really early flight," she added in case they determined the implausibility of the first excuse. "Thank you. It was lovely." She hugged Blanca. "Tell Anthony I said goodbye. It was so nice meeting both of you." Finally she fixed her gaze on Gil the Batman doctor, ignoring the question in his eyes. "So. See you around. In Alaska, I guess."

It was a disjointed statement which mirrored what she was feeling on the inside. She turned on her heel to exit, her head full of "hurry, hurry" so it would drown out anything he might say to stop her. She was still engaged to Alan. Planning to breakup, but engaged. She wasn't like Carole and her "this is how you play the game." She didn't keep one guy on the line until the other was snagged and reeled in. She ducked into a bathroom to have a moment alone and to run through Alan's texts and then, finally, the voicemail. "Scar, please call me. Lexi's taking over the Van Doren account."

No! Not the Van Doren fiftieth anniversary party. That was hers! Everything she'd felt over the past ten months and one week burned through her. Lexi might have been the one with money to contribute to Ambrose and Bloom, but Scarlett had the event that would get their business noticed. She and Amelia Van Doren had all but signed a contract, and Lexi had nothing to do with it. Not then, and especially not anymore.

After depositing the scrubs and the beaver hat at the front desk with a note to Bailey, she marched to her car, hoping Gil wasn't waiting there to ask questions, but also not caring if he was. Getting back to Phoenix was all that mattered.

She rounded the last row of cars, and there he was, back in his regular T-shirt and jeans with traces of black around his eyes, leaning against her Honda. He straightened when she approached. "Are you okay?"

"I'm sorry, Gil. I have kind of an emergency at home. I have to leave right now." Her pulse hummed.

Alarm creased his brow. "Anything I can do?"

"Not the doctor kind of emergency." She smiled halfheartedly at his offer.

"Is it the Batman kind? I'll get my cape." He raised his eyebrows, and she found herself smiling again. Why was he so nice . . . in a T-shirt, in a cape? Why was he . . . gravy?

"Nice T-shirt." His comment startled her, almost as if he had read her thoughts. "You don't miss the parkas and mittens."

CHRISTMAS FUTURE

Mentally she shivered at the thought of the low in Anchorage that day, but there was no time to worry about temperatures and snow and everything else that awaited her next week. She unlocked her car and slid inside to prove her point. She really had to go. "I'll see you up north where the air is chill and my toes are too." She reversed out of the parking spot and then watched him in her rearview watching her as she pulled away.

She flipped on the radio to calm the voices in her head. "Why do I complicate my life?" she said aloud to Ed Sheeran, who was crooning about diving right in and looking perfect. She hit a button to change stations. *Where's love advice from Delilah when you need it?*

But she couldn't worry about Gil and their kiss. She needed to avert a crisis, one that threatened the future of Ambrose Events. Her future. It was the whole reason she was working in Alaska to publicize Christmas spirit, a project that morphed into a Dickens Village, that led her to accidentally meet a professor who was really a handsome doctor. Who was taken! She pounded out a staccato beat on the steering wheel. Why did he kiss her? Did he break up with Carole?

She merged onto I-10 toward Phoenix. *Focus.* She had to have a big starter, something to fill a portfolio. No one would be impressed by the family weddings, two graduation parties, and one bar mitzvah she had helped plan in high school and college. If she didn't have the Van Doren account, her business was doomed.

It was telling that Alan had referred to it as the Van Doren account instead of by his great-aunt's name, Amelia. That's how uppity of an affair their fiftieth was going to be. It would be the kind of event to appear on the nightly news. "Who's your event coordinator?" people would ask. "Scarlett of Ambrose Events, of course."

She would never forget the moment Aunt Amelia approached her at Alan's cousin's wedding almost a year ago. "Clear your calendar, young lady. This has nothing to do with you dating Alan. You're doing my anniversary party," she said. "Everything I love about this wedding seems to have had your hand on it."

They agreed to begin planning in January of next year. That was plenty of time for Scarlett to complete her commitment to the internship and be back in town. *Lexi, what have you done?*

"Call Alan," she instructed her phone, and he picked up immediately.

"Scarlett, I am so sorry. I shouldn't have invited Lexi and T.J. to dinner. I thought about what you said, and I want you to know I cancelled. You were right. I messed up. I'm sorry."

"Alan, stop. Tell me what you know about your Aunt Amelia's event. Did Lexi say something to you?"

"When I told my mom today that you couldn't make the Hawaii trip because of your job in Alaska, she said Aunt Amelia was worried about that. I guess you were supposed to be meeting with her?"

"In January." Scarlett groaned, then checked her speedometer and let up on the gas a bit. *Relax.* There was no time and money for police officers and speeding tickets.

"Then when I called to cancel dinner, Lexi said she'd been talking to my aunt about the anniversary party. That Amelia had called her."

"No. It's not possible. I never gave her Lexi's name. I'm still an hour and a half away, Alan. Do you think eight is too late to show up at her door to discuss this?"

"At Lexi's?"

"No!" She forced a deep breath before repeating more calmly, "No. Your Aunt Amelia's. Could you call her to set it up, and then will you come with me?"

"Of course, babe. I've been wanting to see you all day."

Hold the babe stuff, she wanted to say, but it was not the time.

"I love you," Alan said.

"I'll see you soon." Scarlett ended the call, and then wondered at the moisture that welled up in her eyes. One tear broke free, and the rest followed in an unbroken stream.

Her future. She had it figured out once.

❄

By 8:30 p.m. she was sitting down with Alan, Amelia, and

Great-uncle Sloan in their grand living room that somehow even put Alan's parents' to shame. They sipped tea from gilt-edged cups and consumed slices of pound cake set on white doilies set on matching bone china dessert plates.

"I'm sorry for the mix up," Scarlett began. "I'm the sole owner of Ambrose Events, and I'm looking forward to meeting with you in January to start planning."

Apparently Amelia had been confused when she heard that Scarlett was working in Alaska. "Alan, I believe your mother gave me that Bloom girl's contact information," Amelia stated as innocently as a wide-eyed child.

Scarlett raised her eyebrows at Alan while abruptly setting her plate down on the coffee table. She didn't want to break anything.

"I told her, 'Hold up, Melly,' but she wouldn't listen." Uncle Sloan inserted himself into the conversation, then stuffed half a piece of cake in his mouth before reaching for his cup. "Why are we drinking tea? Got anything stronger around here?"

Scarlett took a breath, just grateful for his presence. As fussy as Amelia was, Sloan was the opposite, laid back, not a care in his moneyed-man's world.

"There must have been a misunderstanding." Alan was giving his mother the benefit of the doubt.

At least one of them would. Scarlett allowed herself another sip from her cup to keep her mouth busy.

Alan continued, "Aunt Melly, Scarlett is who you want, not Lexi."

"Okay, I see. January then. I guess I got overexcited." She poured more tea for everyone, but Scarlett's work was done.

Later she paused with Alan on his relatives' massive, pillared porch to take a breath. She shut everything else out of her mind to focus on the victory. "Thank you. You saved me."

He pulled her close. "Now you'd better deliver."

CHAPTER 17
Anchorage: 29°
Los Angeles: 85°

Everything went well at Loren Medical on Monday with Gil's spur-of-the-moment orientation. But as much as the team seemed thrilled to have him on board, he had a hard time picturing himself there. It was a maze of offices, hallways, and exam rooms, not to mention the gleaming tile floors, expensive artwork on the walls, and high tech everywhere. A massive aquarium took up one wall. The huge children's section of the waiting room was a spoiled, rich kid's dream outfitted with video consoles and two battery-powered ride-on cars, one a black Lamborghini and the other a pink Mercedes Coupe. He watched a brother and sister fight over one of the vehicles and thought how Anthony and his other little patients would have been awed by such a place.

Someone in the office had posted a copy of the online article from late September. *The Compassionate Doctor*, the headline read, *set to join Loren Medical in their new state-of-the-art facility*. He ignored it, along with the many female staffers, young and old, who gushed over him. At least as much as they allowed him to. The article played up the idea that he'd chosen to practice medicine among the poorer areas of the inland county, as if he'd done it for an entry on his resume. They made him out to be some kind of saint when he'd been the beneficiary. His scholarship covered fees and tuition. He'd been able to focus on his studies without the added financial weight of student loans. And in the process, he'd found that he loved the people he served.

Maybe that was what held him back. Fear that his job would

CHRISTMAS FUTURE

become more about a physician's paycheck and less about the people in his care.

Or maybe it was all about location. Loren Medical was in southern California, not any of the places where Scarlett Ambrose might be. His flights from Phoenix to LAX and then back to Anchorage had offered too much time to think. He knew he and Cari had grown in different directions, maybe because they spent so much time apart or they valued different things, and he had, like a guy, according to Scarlett, missed important pieces of the puzzle. But it had nothing to do with her. He didn't even know if their paths would cross again, though her parting words were "I'll see you up north . . ."

He couldn't stop thinking about her. How she interacted with the kids at the Halloween party, but especially about the moment after—and her leaving so abruptly. He'd resisted texting her to see if things were okay at home and to ask how her flight from Arizona went. With the way the night ended, maybe she needed to be the one to reach out first.

He arrived at the college early Tuesday, determined to locate the manuscript, ready his dad's books for their new home in the library, and sort through the rest. The distraction of sorting out relationships would have to wait.

"Hey, Darlene."

"Welcome back, Gil. You tore yourself away from that balmy Arizona weather?"

"It was difficult, but duty called."

"Speaking of calls, a couple more came from London. Seems like the same guy as before. Says he's been trying to reach you."

Gil had left a message over the weekend but ignored the publisher Monday. "I'm sorry they're resorting to calling the college again, but I should have good news for them today."

Back in the office, he recovered the plastic bin that stored yellow legal pads filled with his dad's longhand. As he gave them a second look, he marveled that he hadn't tossed the whole thing because the penmanship was so flowing and nearly illegible. His anticipation deflated. He couldn't submit this to a publisher.

Darlene was a department secretary, not Dad's personal

assistant, but maybe she would have some clues. He grabbed his coat and hat. He wanted to see Nate in IT before leaving the state, so he would stop by Darlene's desk on the way over.

"Did you find the golden ticket?" she kidded when she saw him.

"The golden legal pads, at least, but they're not fit to send to any editor. I think I assumed they'd be readable somehow, but they're a mess. Any ideas?"

"It's possible he paid a service here in town to type it up or maybe a student trying to earn some extra money. I know they get pretty good at deciphering chicken scratch."

Gil sat down on one of the vinyl, standard-issue chairs that lined the wall next to the secretary's desk. "Why do I feel like I'm going in circles here?"

"This has become quite the job, hasn't it? I'm sorry I haven't been much help." The secretary pulled on her coat and gloves, then reached for her purse.

"I don't know what you're talking about, Darlene. You're the one who made the initial arrangements for sending his body home. You hired someone to clear out his townhouse. You have been . . ." He stopped. "The boxes. I haven't looked at the stuff from the townhouse."

"Oh, goodness. I forgot all about those, Gil. I'm leaving early for a doctor's appointment, but you help yourself." She opened a door behind the desk area. "See, in the corner of the storage room with your dad's initials marked on the side? That's them. You might even get lucky and find a laptop with your dad's work already on it."

"I hope so. Thank you."

"Don't thank me and my bad memory," she said. "I should have reminded you about those boxes. Last question. Will I see you tomorrow or do I need to give you a hug right now?"

He crossed the foyer and folded her into a bear hug. "Thank you, Darlene." He pulled back to arm's length. "It makes me feel good knowing my dad had such kind people to work with here. And, yes, I'll see you tomorrow."

"Oh, you." She playfully slapped his shoulder. "If I were twenty years younger. Okay, maybe thirty or thirty-five, but that's just between you and me. Except you're taken."

CHRISTMAS FUTURE

"Between you and me, I'm breaking it off with my girlfriend."

She grasped the edges of her beaver hat and tugged it over her ears. "I'm sorry to hear that, but better to figure it out sooner than later. That means I might have a chance then?"

"Of course. If I were ten years older." He winked at her.

"You're a charmer, Gilbert Pennington," she said before turning toward the exit.

Gil loaded a dolly with three boxes and carted them down the hall, then returned for the last two. Not only did he have hopes for the manuscript, but certainly the carved nativity was among the things his dad would have kept at home.

The first box he opened was a heavy one filled with dishware. He recognized the pattern as one Mom picked out. He smiled to think of his dad going to the trouble of shipping dishes to Alaska. He would check with Izzy to see if she wanted them. The largest box contained clothing, towels, and personal hygiene items, nothing of sentimental value. He tossed most of it. Some could be donated to the Salvation Army. A smaller one held framed family photos: of Mom, of the four of them on a fishing trip, of Izzy and Shawn on their wedding day, and one of Penn as a baby. Izzy had returned to Spokane after cleaning out the California house with the rest of the savable items like photo albums and scrapbooks.

The last two boxes were crammed with books. His dad was definitely an English professor. His personal library proved that. The bottom of one box contained two unopened three-packs of yellow pads. Books left unwritten. Or had Dad decided that four comprised all he wanted to say.

It gave Gil an idea, though. He meticulously thumbed through each of the new titles, and after a dozen or so, he was rewarded with a receipt for a typing service. *Finally some good news.* He stacked both boxes near the door with the others awaiting pickup before grabbing his phone to tap in the number for Elite Business Services. A nice girl answered and confirmed his dad's order. She said the professor had opted for the file to be saved on a flash drive as well as emailed. She even described in detail the small white padded envelope with a red stripe and their logo that the drive would have been mailed in. While on the phone he returned to the plastic bin. "It looks like the legal pads are here. Would it have been mailed back together?"

"Separately," she replied. "We always send the flash drives in the small envelopes so they don't get mixed up with bigger items and lost."

Gil drew out each pad, one at a time, even giving them a quick shake. On the last shake a padded envelope fell out. Inside was a flash drive with a sticker identifying the service. "Thank you so much for your help." He ended the call and collapsed into the desk chair, still clutching the device. *Finally*!

The desktop his dad used was gone and Darlene was out of the office. Time to pay Nate that visit. Gil retrieved his coat and beaver hat before heading out the door. Fortunately Nate was at the counter where Gil had met him before.

"Dr. P's son! How's it going? I thought you'd be long gone by now."

"Me too, but I made a few side trips. I actually went up to Fairbanks and met Ves."

"That's sweet, man. He's a cool dude, huh?"

"Really good people, both him and his wife." Gil placed the padded envelope down in front of him.

"Didn't have the pleasure of meeting her, but, yeah, sweet. What can I do you for?"

"I need to send an email, but I don't have access to a computer."

"Come on back."

Gil inserted the flash drive and brought up the only file it contained. The title popped up on the screen, "The Charles Dickens Letters Project." He logged on to his account, found the address of the publisher, and typed it into a new email. He wrote a quick note and attached the file before hitting send. *Hope this is what you want, Dad.*

After talking to Nate a bit longer, Gil returned to the English department to make another pass through the office. With the shelves emptied and the desk cleared, he finally felt like he was close to wrapping things up.

After grabbing a sandwich from the campus café, he worked on separating piles in a near-empty office: to toss, to donate, to ask Izzy about. A life boiled down to three categories. But the

CHRISTMAS FUTURE

last one, what to save, was the one that mattered. It included the pictures and a certain china pattern, and also every memory that filled his heart. He would have to tell his sister to look for the nativity again among the things she carried home from LA, but even if they never found it, they had the memory of their dad's gift to their mother. They'd been in on the secret, assigned to keep Mom out of his small woodshop while he worked. Dad never considered himself an artist, but he liked working with his hands. He joked it was the reason he became a writer.

Gil lingered over the family photos again. He'd set them up across the desk like witnesses to the last remnants of Dad's life. He picked up Izzy's wedding photo while his mind wandered to the moments not pictured. Mom had been allowed to attend despite her failing health, and even though she lamented the necessity of a wheelchair, she had been present for that milestone event in her daughter's life. She passed within the year and missed the birth of her first grandchild, and the second.

He gathered the frames into their box, determined not to go down that melancholy road. In the back of his mind, he knew both his parents would be absent for his own important events, but he chose to focus on happy memories. He could seek for a marriage like theirs, create a home like theirs where he would tell and retell the family stories.

He shook away the daydream. Izzy survived dividing a home into three piles, but the twelve by twelve space he had undertaken was challenging his sensibilities. He re-dressed in his outerwear for a trek to his car with the dishes, and then a second trip with the items to be donated. He left the box of pictures to give him a reason to come back. He wasn't sure why he'd told Darlene that, but his flight out wasn't until Sunday. Maybe he assumed he could drag it out, or maybe he wasn't ready to be done with Alaska.

He pulled out his phone and made a reservation for two at a nice restaurant known for its spectacular view. Then his ringtone echoed with a call from Cari. They hadn't communicated over the weekend except for a few texts while he sat in airports.

"Guess who's a brand new host on the jewelry show? Tiffany!" she bubbled.

"Congratulations. I know it's what you wanted." His tone

flattened. He was afraid to ask about the timing, but he didn't have to.

"They want me to start after Thanksgiving. I think that's perfect."

"Aren't you doing segments for Christmas Carole through the holidays?"

"There's the big one to introduce the show the day after Thanksgiving, but the rest don't have to be live. I'm going to talk to Hudson. Now what do you think about me being just Tiffany? No last name."

"I don't have an opinion on that."

"Gil," she huffed.

"Cari, I made reservations for dinner."

He could hear her take a breath. "I'm in LA. I flew home Sunday for a third interview with the show yesterday. I should have told you, but I wanted to surprise you with the job. You met with Loren. I got the host gig. Our future's set."

Gil dropped into the upholstered desk chair. If he had known they'd been in California at the same time, he could have given her a beach breakup. He almost laughed out loud at the absurdity of the thought. "There's more than our careers to figure out."

"I know that. I'll start house hunting this week."

"I'm flying out Sunday." A familiar ache moved from his stomach to settle in his chest. How exactly does one break off an engagement?

"That's when I'm flying back up, Gil. I have to be there the week before Thanksgiving. I'll email you a list of questions the wedding planner emailed me."

"Wedding planner? Cari, do you see what's happening? We're like two ships that pass in the night, except we're Alaska Air flights. We should want to be together, not because we have details to work out, but because that's where home is. It doesn't matter if it's in Alaska or California or the middle of a desert."

The phone went quiet, and he wasn't sure if he should fill the space or wait for her reaction. "What are you saying?" she asked finally.

"I love you and the time we've had, but I think I've changed. Blame it on my dad's death, if you want, but I'm looking for different things now. I don't even know if living in southern California is what I want."

"Then I guess I'm glad I found that out now." Cari seemed to be choosing her words carefully.

He was too. "I'm really sorry, Cari. I realize this is not a conversation to have over the phone. I just don't want to mislead you. I'm happy you got the job you wanted. You'll be perfect for it."

"That's what they said when they offered it to me." She laughed, but maybe she was trying to cover. Then she spoke again. "You're right about us. Things haven't been the same for a long time, even before your dad died. Good thing I have options. I'm kidding," she backtracked.

The pain in his chest lessened a bit as they ended the call. He cancelled dinner reservations, palmed the Bah! Humbug! rock into his pocket and left the building.

CHAPTER 18
Anchorage: 28°
Phoenix: 82°

When Scarlett arrived with the snow flurries at her apartment late Tuesday morning, there was no time to huddle under a heap of comforters by a roaring fire to chug hot chocolate. Even soaking in a hot bath with a towel waiting for her on the warmer would have to wait. After missing an unplanned extra day of work, she couldn't even afford the luxury of plugging in the space heater. No matter how deeply the bitter frost dragged at her bones.

She'd almost burst into tears when all twenty-eight degrees of it accosted her as she emerged not appropriately bundled from the airport into a waiting taxi. After two days grounded in Seattle due to ice, wind, fog—whatever it was didn't matter—tears were another indulgence she emotionally did not have time for.

Welcome to Alaska, the Last Frontier." The slogan autoplayed loop after sarcastic loop around her brain. November, and she was still in this state. But she wasn't convinced she would rather be in Arizona either. Despite her having reclaimed the Van Doren account from Lexi's clutches, Alan's response had left her hollow. Not, "You're going to rock the anniversary party," but "Now you'd better deliver." What did he even mean—give Amelia the event she deserved, or did he think she should reward him for his help?

She'd left him hanging after a hurried goodnight. It was true, she had a particularly early flight out the next morning. For what that excuse was worth, three days later.

CHRISTMAS FUTURE

An added sore spot was the purple envelope she'd found stuffed into her purse at some point along her disjointed travel from Arizona. Her mom knew full well that she didn't want to deal with anything Lexi-related, not even a check to pay back her portion. At some point she'd cash it—she wasn't too proud for that—but it would be after Ambrose Events opened on its own. Without any payback from Bloom.

After growling at the heater and starting the coffee pot, she returned to her abandoned bag just inside the front door. She unzipped it to grab some essentials and then headed to a quick, very hot shower. If she hurried, she might avoid the snow becoming her nemesis on the drive to work. Her limited sleep at the airport and on the plane would have to suffice because she had an appointment with Micki Blanding to survey the handpicked site for the Dickens Village.

When the elevator doors opened on the foyer of the Department of Commerce, Community, and Economic Development, something was missing.

The tree.

In its place was a scarecrow on a post against a backdrop of corn husks. Pumpkins filled in the area around the base. Absolutely no garland circled the cubicle city, and no one called out Merry Christmas. Instead someone actually said "Welcome back, Scarlett," though the tone seemed off, worried or nervous somehow. In four days someone had razed Christmas and then raised Thanksgiving in its place. For that she would be grateful.

"Scarlett!" Trina grabbed her in a bear hug the moment she entered their office space. "I was afraid you might never come back, but you're here, you're here."

She waited for Trina to finish before pulling off her outerwear bit by bit. Impulsively she plucked the Lexi-envelope from her purse and shoved it deep within the heap before closing everything into the drawer. She was draping her coat on a hook when Daniel appeared in the cubicle opening.

"Hey, Scarlett. Rough flight, huh?"

"Not as rough as that twenty-eight degree greeting." She couldn't even muster a smile. Maybe because she wasn't kidding.

"Great job with North Pole, by the way, and I negotiated

with Mayor Blanding to send someone to pick you up this afternoon so you don't have to drive in the snow."

"Thanks, Daniel. Best news I've had all week." She'd still have to wander outside in the snow making plans for what went where, but she would survive. Probably.

"Well, it's only Tuesday." A concerned look furrowed his brow, and Scarlett thought she detected the exchange of glances between him and Trina.

"Don't remind me." She groaned before Daniel stepped away without saying anything else.

Trina wasn't done gushing. "It's been forever, Scarlett. You haven't been in the office since last Tuesday. Tell me everything. How was Arizona?"

"Arizona is a magical world where you can wear T-shirts in October," she stated. *Don't mention T-shirts.*

"How's Alan?" When Scarlett didn't immediately respond to the question, Trina ventured. "Are you still engaged?"

Scarlett held up her left hand to show her ring, but it felt like admitting defeat.

Trina frowned. "Well, great to see you so happy about it. What happened?"

Scarlett attempted to cover a weary sigh. "I have a lot of work to do before I meet with the mayor. Can we talk about it later?"

Concern crisscrossed Trina's face. "Are you okay?"

Gil asked her that same question Saturday night, and she had wanted to reply, *I was okay until I kissed this really hot doctor that I might be falling in love with and I'm still engaged and trying to figure out what I should do, and, and . . .* It was too complicated. She could only nod her head yes to her friend's question. It wasn't a lie if she didn't speak it out loud.

Trina huffed. "Fine. Go back to being a lump of coal if you want. I mean, you got your wish. Someone tore down all the Christmas decorations, though beware of the break room, there's a mangled Christmas tree in the corner. And I'll even keep my Jingle Bells and Silent Night to myself."

"What did you say?"

"Okay, sorry. Maybe I was kidding when I called you a lump of coal."

"No, after that. Jingle Bells and Silent Night?"

"Yeah, so?"

"Nothing, never mind." Scarlett palmed her mouse to wake up her computer. "I really do have a lot of work to do, but when this is all over, we'll talk. Deal?"

Trina grabbed her around the shoulders from behind. "I'm so glad you came back. Let's take an early coffee break so we can talk now."

Scarlett was tempted. She had to tell someone about what happened in Arizona or she'd burst, but work first.

"I can't Trina." Scarlett dismissed her friend's suggestion and opened her inbox to scroll. Trina was acting overly dramatic, even for her.

"I'm sorry, Scarlett. I knew it was no use trying to distract you." Trina wrapped her arms around for one more hug.

Distract me? Her brother Royce's name caught her attention, and she immediately clicked on the email. *"What's up with this?"* she read. Under his question he linked to a blog post written by a popular blogger who addressed topics of local entertainment, fashion, nightlife, and general human interest stories.

The headline stopped her cold. *Is Alaska's Christmas Spirit Campaign Led by a Scrooge?*

❄

Scarlett couldn't keep from comparing Mayor Blanding to Mayor Sprouse. There were physical differences, but spending a couple of hours with Micki Blanding, a bug-eyed, wiry ball of energy who talked nonstop until Scarlett finally just agreed, had her longing for Glenda Sprouse's more understated manner even though the woman did speak bluntly at times. Or all the time.

Or maybe she was distracted by a certain blog post that had nothing to do with Micki Blanding whatsoever. Or was it the conversation she overheard on her way to the break room: "I know why her hair's so curly." "Why?" "Let's just say she's a little tightly wound."

Was it pathetic that she wanted to straighten her hair for work the next morning? As if that was going to somehow make everything they said about her untrue. That she wasn't really a Scrooge. She could expect more than a stocking full of coal for Christmas. *Right.*

She and the mayor traversed the site just outside Charlestown with Micki calling out "parade route here, booths there, stage here, sleigh rides over there" while Scarlett counted off toes as they succumbed to numbness. Lips and nose were next, though she kept a gloved hand to her face as much as possible. Micki didn't expect anything but nodding.

"Where would you like Santa Claus?" Scarlett asked when they arrived back where they started. *See? It was not a question a Scrooge-like person would care about.*

"Father Christmas?" Micki corrected. "He'll be on the stage, of course, across from the booths. Remember I pointed it out?"

That was probably about toe ten, and the numbing must have affected her hearing. But she hadn't missed when the mayor asked at least three times, "You have Dickens carolers lined up, don't you?" *Carolers? Oh, boy, do I have carolers.* Unfortunately Micki had ideas bigger than the budget and the available time, and these were sticking points for Scarlett.

Okay, maybe I am a Scrooge, set in my ways when it comes to money.

When she could thaw her vocal cords, she forced the two points. The mayor appeared undeterred. "I have a good feeling about you. You're someone who is not afraid of hard work. I think you can do anything you set your mind to."

She means anything she *sets my mind to.* But flattery and empty clichés did not a Dickens Village make.

On the drive back to the office, Scarlett warmed up with the car's heater and fielded calls from Heath, who was ready to finalize plans for a surprise engagement party for Trina. His use of the word finalize caused a bit of whiplash. They'd talked once at Ruby's, but apparently he'd taken her at her word when she said she was available "next week," after she got back from Arizona. In fact he took her so literally that he'd set up a private online group and invited friends and family to an event Saturday night at his mom's apartment complex in Wasilla. At least the venue was secured.

CHRISTMAS FUTURE

Through multiple calls while Heath helped customers at the pet store, Scarlett finally comprehended that he had made it easy for her. His best friend was on tap to run a paid bar, and his cousin would DJ. His mom and sister had already started making palm trees out of cardboard and tissue paper. He really did just need help with food. When they settled on a menu, she knew she needed to broach the subject of the ceremony again.

"Heath, can I just say something about—" she began.

"The paid bar? Is it tacky?" he interrupted.

"No, it's fine. I mean, you know your friends and family. I don't. It makes sense because you've invited a lot of people." A lot of people who were going to be witness to an engagement-party fail if he didn't change his mind about announcing a destination wedding in Hawaii.

"That's an understatement."

It took a moment to realize his reply was a response to what she'd said out loud, not to what she had been thinking. "Actually I was going to bring up the red church in Seward. You realize how much Trina—"

He interrupted again. "Don't worry. You forget that I know her. I got this. Oops, another customer. I'm out."

What do you got? Scarlett wanted to yell into the phone, but he was gone. At least he hadn't mentioned the blog post, so maybe the entire world hadn't read it yet. Her instinct was to text Gil to see what advice he'd have for round two with Heath. Instead she buried the phone in her bag and made her way to Daniel's office to hash out all the ways she couldn't fulfill the Dickens Village of Micki Blanding's dreams.

Somehow she made headway on the project, despite the fact that her own plans didn't quite mesh with the mayor's. By Friday she had informed the carpenters of changes and hired a Father Christmas. *Not Santa Claus.* Micki's lilting voice played like a rerun in her head. She also put off the printer for another week. That was no small feat because they were near their drop-dead print time to be able to get the entry forms ready to distribute by Thanksgiving weekend. She hadn't settled on a name for the campaign because she wasn't feeling settled in general. Going a mile a minute since landing at the airport didn't lend itself to quiet reflection.

Nor did persistent thoughts of Gil. She hoped spilling the whole crazy thing to Trina midweek would somehow make them go away, but, of course, Trina took way too much delight in every detail. His name seemed on the fringe of nearly every conversation in their cubicle since then.

Saturday she was grateful for the distraction of shopping and food prep for the engagement party. She'd done what she could to prepare Trina without giving away the surprise. Hopefully her subtle reminders of "Heath really does love you" and "Keep an open mind when you discuss wedding decisions" sank in. Her friend didn't question anything Scarlett said since it came from the mouth of an event planner. Still, as she shredded chicken and chopped vegetables all afternoon, she worried she hadn't said enough.

After her prior weekend in Phoenix, driving to Wasilla in the dark at barely 5:00 p.m. felt strange. She'd been warned about the lack of sunlight, that it lessened a bit each day. Certainly this was no place for a girl from the Valley of the Sun.

At the clubhouse, Heath's mom and sister helped her set up Hawaiian Haystacks, buffet-style, on a counter wrapped in a grass table skirt. A rented tiki bar claimed a space close to the kitchen. Surfboard cutouts sporting the letters A-L-O-H-A adorned one wall, and gaudy crepe-paper hibiscus and palm fronds covered everywhere else. And then there were the trees, of course. Thankfully Amelia Van Doren wouldn't have to know anything about this.

Soon the guests took up their semihidden posts to wait for Heath to arrive with Trina. To distract herself, Scarlett lamented the use of canned pineapple and hoped the rice and chicken gravy weren't getting cold—anything to dismiss her worry about what would happen when Heath got the microphone in his hand.

Excited whispers of "they're here, they're here," swelled like a wave around the room, and the couple entered amid shouts of "Surprise."

Before Trina even realized it was an engagement party, Scarlett was startled by the unexpected appearance of a certain doctor coming in the clubhouse door behind them. She did the only mature thing she could think of. She ducked into the kitchen, which was nowhere to hide since it was divided from

CHRISTMAS FUTURE

the rest of the space by only a long curved counter. She busied herself at the sink, though, starting water and soap for dirty dishes. Her avoidance wasn't destined to last because her friend pointed Gil in that direction.

He appeared at her elbow. "You also have skills with grass skirts and tiki torches?" he asked, a tip of his head indicating the room.

"I only take credit for the food." She slid some utensils into the soapy water.

"Can we talk outside?"

"I have to watch the table in case anything runs out." She wondered if it would be too awkward to take a half step to the right to put space between them. She hadn't come to terms with the idea of kissing him, with the idea of him in general. *Why does someone so perfectly nice want to hang out with the resident Scrooge?*

"They haven't started to eat yet." Gil pointed out the obvious.

"A good hostess doesn't leave her post." Scarlett's thoughts wandered to her short conversation with his fiancée in the parking garage at KWIX last week. Gil deserved better than Christmas Carole.

"I was worried after you left Saturday. Is everything okay at home?"

They were still standing shoulder to shoulder, speaking but not looking at each other, and with long pauses in between sentences. No one would even know they were having a conversation unless they saw their mouths moving every once in a while. "I had to save the Van Doren account," she replied.

"And that is?"

"A fiftieth anniversary event. Lexi, the Bloom half of our former business, tried to get her hands on it. It's all Ambrose Events has." She pasted on a smile when she noticed Trina watching her. "You know me, putting business first." *Before love. Like Linus in* Sabrina. She felt a flush creep up her cheeks. Hopefully Gil didn't have the same thought.

"You're sure you don't want to go outside and talk?" Gil asked again.

She was saved by Heath, who was in a hurry to reveal the

reason for the night. He took the mike and led his fiancée to the area in front of the Aloha surfboards. Surely, in Alaska they didn't care about fresh pineapple, and Scarlett had set the rice cookers back on warm. She worried about Trina.

Heath talked about how they met at the pet store and how her fish, Marley, the multiple Marleys, kept dying, and he was getting suspicious. "It was about Marley number six or seven, I forget, that I knew I really liked her and wanted to be with her," he said, and everyone laughed. "Then something big happened, and I knew it was a sign that I should ask her to marry me. Trina, I won a trip to Hawaii."

From her post behind the kitchen counter, Scarlett zeroed in on Trina's face as her friend's jaw went slack and her eyebrows twisted.

"Did you talk to him again?" Gil mumbled under his breath, but Scarlett could only nod.

Heath dropped to one knee and reached behind to where his DJ cousin was handing him a lei. Not the beautiful, flowery kind, but a dollar store version. Scarlett gripped the counter, afraid for his next words. "Trina, will you marry me on the beach in Hawaii. If you don't, I'll have to let my mom use the other ticket." Everyone laughed again as she nodded her head and leaned down, as if on cue, to accept the lei around her neck. Heath stood. They kissed. Everyone applauded while Scarlett tried to gauge Trina's quick tears? Happy or horrified? But she knew all too well what it felt like when she'd said yes after Alan's big production. A little bit of both.

"Wait, wait." Heath wasn't done. "I want to thank some people. First, Trina's Uncle Frank for giving me a job at the pet store so I could meet her. Well, maybe first I should thank Trina's mom for having her." Groans filled the room. Trina recovered enough to steal the mike away. "Heath told me that Scarlett planned the party. We should be thanking her."

"I was getting to that," Heath leaned in to say.

"Just the food, just the food," Scarlett said in her defense, but they clapped all the louder at what they presumed was her humility. She stole a look at Gil, who appeared to be fighting a smile.

She elbowed him in the side. "What are you doing here,

anyway?" Trina had handed the microphone back to Heath, so he could continue his thank you list.

"I'm not laughing at you. Just the whole situation is kind of comical, don't you think? And what are the odds, Heath's mom works at the hotel I'm staying at? She was sitting at the front desk cutting out palm leaves this week, so naturally I was curious. I forgot that you told me it was a surprise party or I would have been here early."

"Why do I get the feeling you're mocking me? You don't even know Heath or Trina."

He reached for her hand. "But I knew you would be here, Scarlett. I guess I need to know if there's any reason I shouldn't get on a plane in the morning and fly back to California."

She was pretty sure her hand warmed to his touch because there was no doubt the rest of her body did. She drew her attention back to the Aloha surfboards when she heard Trina's voice again. "I'm really lucky to have a friend like Scarlett Ambrose," she was saying. "I hope she'll be my wedding planner, if she's not too busy planning her own wedding, of course."

Gil dropped her right hand and reached for the other, zeroing in on her ring before letting it fall back to her side. "You're still engaged? But what about your text? I wouldn't have kissed you if I'd known you didn't break it off."

Adrenaline flared, but she wouldn't look at him. "Then what does that say about you? As of last weekend you were still engaged, weren't you?"

"I know, but I was making a plan to change that."

"Well, don't do anything on my account. You don't kiss girls that are engaged, and I don't kiss guys that are engaged. So I guess it never happened."

Gil lowered his voice. It was hard to hear above the noise of guests at the buffet table. "Can we please talk outside?"

"This is a great party, honey. Two, I mean, two thumbs up." A woman with a drink in her hand fumbled with her thumbs.

Scarlett fake-smiled in response, but inside, her mind raced and her heart ached with wanting to tell him how she really felt. How she was making plans to break up too. *But how dare he be so accusatory?* "Lucky for your fiancée you weren't so overcome with Halloween spirit that you proposed to me right then and there." She knew it was wrong to use his own words against him, but he was wrong to be so hypocritical. *I shouldn't have kissed him, but he shouldn't have kissed me either!*

She relaxed her hands, which had tightened into fists, and fought to control her breathing. Somehow the conversation about proposals while stuck in Gil's dad's office seemed so long ago. Not waiting for him to reply, Scarlett grabbed hot pads and lifted a pot off the stove. "If you'll excuse me, I think the gravy is running low.

CHAPTER 19
Anchorage: 34°
Los Angeles: 78°

Flying from a hotel in Alaska to a hotel in California. What was the difference? The thought weighed on Gil's mind as he sat buckled into his aisle seat aboard the Alaska Air flight to LAX. He preferred it to the discussion going on between the two women next to him. They were laughing and lamenting the fact that they'd never witnessed one of those airport scenes out of a movie where the girl's leaving and the guy comes running down the concourse like a crazy person in love and the door shuts and he's too late, but then someone taps him on the shoulder and it's her and she couldn't leave because she loves him too. Or vice versa.

It happened only in movies. It certainly didn't happen that morning at Ted Stevens International in Anchorage. Because if there was any way possible that Scarlett was sneaking past airport security and dodging luggage-bearing passengers to come after him, he wouldn't have boarded the plane. Yeah, only in movies.

He pulled up the photos of them in North Pole with the various festive street signs, pausing at the one on Mistletoe Drive. It was his favorite because of the contrast between the twilight sky and the glow of her smile. How does a girl get under a person's skin and into their heart so quickly? And why was he heading in the opposite direction from where she was?

Because she was engaged. That small detail.

He gazed at the picture for a long time, careful to keep it

away from view of the women next to him. He didn't need to spark more conversations about impossible relationships.

He started a long text to his sister to give a final report of his time spent in Alaska. Minus a few highlights.

CHAPTER 20
Anchorage: 27°
Phoenix: 80°

"Daniel, the logistics for the Dickens Village are a nightmare. Micki wants sleigh rides, but the area's not big enough. No one has considered parking. The coffee sponsor has backed out because it's too late to get permission from corporate." Another week had flown by, and instead of progress, plans were falling apart.

"But you have carolers, right, Scarlett?" He screwed his mouth into a grin.

"Lots and lots of carolers." It had become their sardonic mantra because on most days it felt like that was all she had.

He ran a hand across his jaw before speaking. "Maybe you should take a break from Charlestown."

What? "Are you kidding, Daniel? It's November 16th. I don't foresee even sleeping in the next two weeks."

"I mean focus on the publicity for the Christmas spirit project. The graphics are beautiful. Just slap a title on the whole thing and shoot it off to the printer. With that weight off the rest will fall into place."

"Because that's the first rule of event planning. Don't worry, everything will fall into place." Scarlett paced the room. She was too wired to sit.

"'There's no place like home for the holidays.' Everyone loves that slogan."

She stopped in front of him. "Because it's everywhere. I heard it on the radio for a mattress store just this morning."

"When do you do your first segment recordings at KWIX?"

"The day after Thanksgiving."

"And that's the day the publicity rolls out?"

"Yep. Printer drop-*deader* date is Monday. They've been really patient, though I think they would fire me if they could."

"Okay, take a couple hours off. Go for a drive. Do something fun. Maybe even one of the activities listed on the entry form. Let your brain rest."

"I'm walking out of your office right now, and I'm going to pretend you did not just say all the things that you just said." She tapped her index finger on his desk, beating out the rhythm of her words.

"Scarlett." Daniel had his elbows up, and he was rubbing his temples with his fingers.

"Your future is not on the line here. Mine is," she said. "This Scrooge has to prove herself."

He raised his hands in defeat. "Then let us know what we can do to help. As always."

Back in her cubicle, she buried herself in loose ends in an effort to stop the unraveling. There were other coffee places. Parking and sleigh rides were not such easy fixes, but she could do hard things. After all, she'd survived Alaska for four months.

She heard Trina's shuffle behind her and the squeak of her chair as she sat. "Be careful. The Scrooge is in," Scarlett said. "Just warning you."

"You're fine," Trina said, and then nothing.

Scarlett whirled in her seat. "You never come into the office this quiet." Then she noticed her friend's pale cheeks and swollen eyes. "Trina! What's wrong."

Her lip trembled. "Me and Heath broke up."

"No. I'm so sorry." Scarlett scooted her chair over until they were knee to knee and she could grasp both Trina's hands. "What happened? And if you say it was because of the wedding venue, I'm giving up event-planning because that means I screwed up on the number-one most important decision."

"Scarlett, no, stop. Heath told me how you tried to set him straight before the engagement party, but we actually talked about it and decided to marry in Seward and honeymoon in Hawaii, so it wasn't that. It was other things." She sighed. "It was a mutual decision, but that doesn't make it any easier."

Scarlett moved her hands to Trina's shoulders. "You're coming over tonight, or, um, sometime this week, and we'll binge-watch Hallmark movies. Sorry, I wish I could commit, but work is crazy."

"I know, Scrooge. I get it. Is there anything I can help you with?" It was a term of endearment the way Trina said it.

"Yes, please stop me before I use 'There's no place like home for the holidays' for the Christmas campaign."

When Friday morning awoke without the predicted overnight snowfall, Scarlett took it as a sign that she should drive up to Charlestown to meet with Micki Blanding in person again. Sometimes bad news was better understood that way. And Scarlett had plenty of it.

She added long johns to her wardrobe choice and pulled on her new warmer coat, boots, and gloves. The snowplows and sanders had been busy all week, as evidenced by the piles of dirty snow everywhere. Gratefully the roads were clear, and traffic was light, as she headed north out of the city in the dark. The sun was nowhere to be seen and it was already 8:00 a.m.

Despite a growing to-do list, her mind déjàvued to memories of driving the same stretch of highway up to the college. Less then a month had passed since she showed up at the English department in search of Professor Pennington and information about Dickens. Instead she found Gil, a handsome doctor who sometimes dressed as Batman. She hadn't minded being stuck with him in an office or on a road trip. And she'd found him again and again as fate seemed to thrust them together from North Pole all the way to Arizona.

But he was engaged, and he was a hypocrite. She shouldn't have been wasting brain cells on him.

She negotiated the turnoff to Charlestown, determined to focus on her meeting with the mayor. Snow movers were busy at the future site of the Dickens Village as she drove by, but she continued into town to meet Micki at a local coffee shop. Scarlett walked down Main Street, feeling warm and *smug* in her new winter wear. Picturesque storefronts beckoned her: eateries, sweet shops, and antique stores, even a charming bed and breakfast over a used bookstore.

After crossing at the corner, she passed another antique store and a holiday boutique boasting Christmas year-round, before ducking into A Fresh Tart, a quaint, new establishment that wafted the heady smells of coffee, fruit, and baked goodness.

"Scarlett!" Micki waved her over to a corner table where she sat with an open laptop and a cup of tea.

"Thank you for meeting me, Mayor Blanding. There just seems too much to try to cover over the phone," Scarlett explained. A server approached, then retreated with an order for strawberry tartlets and coffee. "This place is darling. Your entire main street is."

"You'd better believe the town council and I have been attentive to the needs of downtown. I campaigned on that, and I delivered." As she spoke, her eyes constantly roamed the room, and she randomly broke out in a smile, or winked and waved at those she saw. It was an effort in concentration for Scarlett, who was only trying to follow her words.

"We've been rewarded with bigger crowds in the summer, but in winter it's a different story," Micki continued. "That's why the Dickens Village will happen. We'll lose retailers if we don't act this season. Do you realize that where we're sitting was a fine art shop and gallery last month? And sure it's busy today, but only because it's the grand opening." She stopped what sounded like a reelection campaign speech to take a sip of tea. Scarlett had heard much of it before, so she dove into the pause.

"Have you seen the report about parking?" She launched into all the issues related to the project while the mayor negated every single one. The delicious tarts proved to be the only positive note about the entire morning.

"You do realize that if we had more time it could really be done right," Scarlett ventured.

"We're not opposed to making improvements in future years," the mayor countered.

"But funding is an issue this year."

Micki paused mid-tartlet. Scarlett's words had come out

more pointedly than intended, and suddenly she was feeling as tightfisted as Scrooge. True, it wasn't her money, but she was responsible for how it was spent. She slowly drained her coffee in an effort to decompress while Micki fidgeted with the last of the strawberry tart without responding. A cute young couple with a baby bundled warmly in a sherpa body sling took seats at the table next to them. Other customers waited in line for coffee and sweets to go.

Scarlett set her cup down and took a breath, the current list of insurmountable issues pressing on her chest. "It almost seems a waste having the carpenters build main street fronts, when you have the real thing right here in downtown." She hadn't meant for it to sound sarcastic, but that wouldn't be at all far from what she was feeling.

"What would be a waste is to get the hopes of all these retailers up and then not deliver," Micki said.

Always has to have the last word. Scarlett fumed all the way back to the office.

"The last Marley has died," Trina announced when Scarlett entered the cubical. "I think I'm over Heath."

"Not yet you're not." She pulled off her hat and tossed it toward her desk, but missed. "We have plans to stay up all night with ice cream and chick flicks. I can do it tonight and tomorrow night and the next night. Don't take this away from me, Trina."

"Wow, whiplash." Trina grabbed her head in a theatrical gesture. "What about work?"

Scarlett groaned. "Can I forget about work?"

"I hate to be the one to tell you this, but it's the weekend before Thanksgiving."

"I know," she barked. "All I can afford to do is work." She collapsed in her chair without finishing her usual outerwear-removal routine.

"That's the Scarlett I know and love." Trina swiveled Scarlett's seat a half turn, then started with the gloves, pulling them off a finger at a time. She unwound the scarf, retrieved the hat from the floor, and shoved them all into the proper drawer.

"Okay, Trina, spill, as you are fond of saying. You've had a crush on Heath since forever. You recently agreed to marry him. So how is this possible?"

"It's weird, but I think he was better as a crush. Then our conversations could revolve around Marley and fish, and that was enough."

Scarlett slid out of her coat at Trina's bidding. "That's deep and very mature. I couldn't bear the thought of eating ice cream, anyway. I was going to change it to hot chocolate and anything else that's in the hot department. Like tarts. I had the best strawberry tart this morning."

"I have never used the word tart in a sentence, much less eaten one."

"They were delicious, Trina. We've got to have some before I fly home. That is, if I ever get this job done." She slumped forward and dropped her hands to her snow boots. "Deliver. That's all I have to do. Just deliver. Deliver a Dickens Village. Deliver a spot on the top-ten list. But really, Alaska's Christmas spirit index would rise if the resident Scrooge left the state, don't you think?" She teased her fingers through her unruly waves, no doubt increasing the mess her hat had made of them.

"Scarlett, leave the drama to me and snap out of this."

Scarlett righted herself and worked at smoothing down her hair. "Are you going to slap me?"

"No, why would I do that?"

"That's what they do in the movies to people who have lost all sensibility, remember? I think that was me last spring when my brother texted me about an exciting adventure with a fat paycheck." She groaned. "Hey, what's that on your desk by the door? Are you hoarding marshmallows for winter?" A zipper baggie full of them had been placed next to the hula girl.

"Those aren't mine. Wait, what? How did I not notice this?"

"What?"

"This note. It's from Fisher."

"What now?"

"No. It's actually kind of sweet." She leaned against the edge of the desk.

"Fisher? Sweet? This I gotta see." Scarlett moved from her chair to Trina's side. "What does it say?"

"I think he's inviting me to a family Christmas party. 'My family gathers every third Saturday in November to kick off the

CHRISTMAS FUTURE

Christmas season. It's not Hawaii, but the campfire, hot chocolate, and good company make it really warm. Fisher.'"

"You're not thinking about going are you? Don't get me wrong. He's nice. He's cute. But he's Fisher."

"But how thoughtful is he, knowing that I just broke it off with Heath and that I'm not going to Hawaii. No-o-o . . . I broke up with a guy that was going to take me to Hawaii. What am I thinking?"

"Don't go there, Trina."

"I know, I know." She sat down to read the note again. And again. When she looked up, Scarlett didn't like the glimmer in her eyes. "So you'll come with me to Fisher's party?"

"Talk about whiplash. Where did I enter into this equation?"

"You need a break from work."

"You know I can't."

"C'mon, every Scrooge needs their great unscrooging. Okay, that sounded really bad, but you know what I mean. Come have some fun. And hot chocolate. You just said you needed hot chocolate."

"Campfires imply outdoors. I don't do outdoors in Alaska in November."

"I'm ignoring that because I happen to know you just bought long johns. Plus you've been moping around even worse than usual because it's been three weeks since you kissed the handsome Dr. P and you won't end it with Alan when it's obvious that you need to."

"I do not mope."

"I'm just trying to put a positive spin on it."

Great. Moping was as positive as Trina could muster.

"Admit it, Scarlett. I'm right. Remember you just said I was the mature one?"

"To be fair, I said you were mature. It wasn't a comparison between the two of us."

"But just like Heath was great crush material, maybe Alan was better as a boyfriend, not a fiancé. I'm sorry, but I can't ignore the signs. I saw them in myself after I got engaged to Heath."

"What do you mean signs? You were engaged for twelve and a half minutes!" She flopped forward again. "Sorry, Trina.

That came out so rude." She whole-body exhaled before straightening again. "I'm going to break off our engagement, you know that, but it's on a long list of things I have to get done."

Trina flashed a look that was a cross between alarm and concern. "Do you hear yourself? This is weighing you down."

Scarlett stirred her seat from side to side. "You sound like Daniel. If I agree to go with you to Fisher's party, will you drop the subject?"

"Fine. But only because I want someone to go with." Trina bent to dig into the drawer where Scarlett kept her gloves and hat. "Is this the envelope from Lexi?"

"Trina, stop."

"You told me Lexi dropped off a purple envelope for you and that you left it unopened at your parents' house." She held it up. "Obviously you brought it back with you, so open it."

"No." Scarlett tried to snatch it out of her hands. "Trina."

"I want to know if there's a check in here or not."

"She told my mom there is. And I didn't bring it back on purpose."

"Is it just the money or is there an apology too? Aren't you dying of curiosity?"

Scarlett stood up. "You must not have much experience with betrayal. I don't want her apology."

"So that's what you're afraid of." Trina moved closer to her desk, keeping the envelope out of reach.

"No. I just don't want that tainted money to have any part of starting my business." Scarlett held out her hand.

"You need an intervention," Trina said before giving up the envelope.

"Now who's being rude?" Scarlett stuffed it back in the drawer.

CHAPTER 21
Los Angeles: 63°
Anchorage: 25°

A fine drizzle early Friday evening meant the beach was mostly clear. As Gil jogged, he dodged a man walking his dog and passed a gray-haired couple strolling hand in hand. He'd finally taken his sister's advice and given up his couch-potato ways of the previous week. She said he needed time to mourn the end of his relationship with Cari, but not with pizza and cable news shows all day, every day. Except maybe mourning the loss of a potential relationship with Scarlett seemed closer to the truth.

He considered his place between jobs, between feeling settled. He had booked yet another hotel room late Sunday night after his flight from Anchorage, this one in Malibu. Running provided time to reflect on rented beds, rental cars, and buying clothes on an as-needed basis. His athletic shorts and thin waterproof running jacket were purchases made this afternoon. Talk about downsizing. He hadn't lived with many personal possessions while practicing in Riverside County, in fact, scrubs were his daily uniform, but reality was hitting him square in the face. He needed a car, a house, a bed, maybe a couch, and a decent wardrobe. His own toilet paper.

"Come keep Christmas with us," Izzy had said when they spoke that morning. *Keeping Christmas.* It had been practically a family motto ever since he could remember. His mom's interpretation of keeping Christmas well meant they were blessed with both the joyful noise and the thoughtful quiet of the season. On nights leading up to Christmas Day, he would often find her sitting on the couch enjoying the multicolored glow of tree lights and the sound of a CD of sacred carols. Even with Christmas cards to write, cookies to bake for neighbors, and presents to wrap, she always took time for a silent night.

He thought he'd found it with Cari. She was beautiful and had a lot of big dreams, and when she buzzed into the hospital last year with all those gifts for the kids, he thought he was smitten for good. Even his dad kept mentioning how thoughtful she was. Gil didn't have the heart to tell him that he found out later she'd paid for them with her dad's credit card and had them gift-wrapped.

One thing he knew for sure, spending Christmas alone was no way to keep it well.

CHAPTER 22
Anchorage: 21°
Phoenix: 68°

Scarlett shivered as Trina leaned in to improve her field of vision over the steering wheel. "Crappy windshield wipers," her friend said. There was just enough precipitation to require their use.

"I'm glad you broached the subject because I think I agreed to let you drive before I had complete information. Your heater is . . . well, is this the best it can do?"

Trina laughed. "Go ahead, say it's crappy. I don't mind."

"Actually I want to call it something worse than crappy, but my mother taught me that even that word doesn't sound sweet coming out of one of her children's mouths."

"That explains everything. When you moved into my cubicle last summer, I was glad you didn't have a mouth like the last woman I shared with"—she shuddered visibly—"but I've never heard you swear, ever. So what would your mom say instead?"

"She would say, cheese and crackers, it's cold in here."

"'Cheese and crackers, it's cold in here'?" Trina snorted and then couldn't stop laughing for several minutes. "That's the best thing I've ever heard. Is that what you've been mumbling under your breath ever since you set foot in Alaska? Cheese and crackers, it's cold. Cheese and crackers, North Pole just hung up on me. Cheese and crackers, the governor wants a cheese and crackers Victorian Village."

"Are you done?" Scarlett gave her a side-eyed look.

159

"I can't believe I'm just now learning this about you, Scarlett. And no, I'm not done. Cheese and crackers, that hot doctor is gravy!"

Scarlett shook her head. "Ignoring that one. What about my question about the heater?"

"Oh, cheese and crackers, the heater." Trina said. "You've got twenty-eight layers on, right? You're good."

Scarlett changed the subject. "Does Fisher think this is a date?"

"Don't be ridiculous. I told him I was bringing you and we were driving up together. Now can I ask you to do something?" Trina didn't take her eyes off the road.

"Does my answer matter?"

"Not really. But I want you to listen before you—"

"I hate conversations that start like that."

"This isn't about Alan or Gil, okay?"

"I'm listening."

"Fisher said his family has a tradition at their annual party. At the end of the night, they take pieces of paper and each person writes down a past hurt or sorrow from the year and then they let it go by throwing it into the fire. It's a physical symbol of what they are doing emotionally. It prepares them to embrace the Christmas season with a whole heart. Isn't that beautiful?"

"That sounds like a lovely tradition." Scarlett monitored the view outside her passenger window. The houses were few and far between, and she was afraid for where Trina's sermonizing was heading.

"Scarlett, you know I'm your friend." Trina reached into her purse and the purple envelope appeared. "I'm sorry, I had to do it. Open it."

Scarlett took it and let out a slow breath.

They didn't passed any sign of civilization for several miles, then a mecca of never-ending multicolored lights, blow up snowmen, and ornamental deer heralded the way to a rambling ranch house. A sturdy, painted wood nativity scene shared a spot near the road with a mammoth-sized wooden moose.

Neither spoke until Trina found a place close and put the car in park. "Scarlett, it's your Ghost of Christmas Past. It will haunt you all through the holidays and beyond that, if you let it."

CHRISTMAS FUTURE

Scarlett considered her options, and throwing the envelope into the fire later was one of them. But Trina was waiting. "Just don't tell me it's for my own good," Scarlett said. "In fact, you open it. You're the one that's so curious."

Trina retrieved it without hesitation, probably to keep Scarlett from changing her mind. "I'll beware of paper cuts," she joked. She slid open the flap and pulled out a card with a field of sunflowers across the front.

"Our favorite flower," Scarlett stated without emotion. Besides the cheery note of "Hello, Sunshine!" printed inside there was a cashier's check and a handwritten letter.

Trina's eyes went wide, and her jaw slacked. "Are you kidding me, Scarlett? This is your portion?"

Scarlett took the check and joined in Trina's shock, but it looked legit. Lexi's signature was there in black ink.

Her friend passed her the letter. "You should read it. Wait, there's a picture." She drew it out of the envelope and after a quick inspection passed it too.

Scarlett's eyes glistened without warning. She and Lexi posing in their maroon caps and gowns after they graduated last December. On the back Lexi had written in her loopy style: *Ambrose & Bloom! We did it!* Scarlett unfolded the letter and began to read.

Scarlett, first let me explain the check. It's your part, plus half of my part (I owe you at least that much after what I did), plus the refund on the space in Scottsdale. I was able to find someone to take over the contract, so we won't have to worry about paying that anymore.

The revelation stopped her. If the contract ended in March, she had a call to make to the bank. On the next line, Lexi began her apology. Scarlett folded the letter back into fourths and returned it to the envelope to read later. The amount of the check still stunned her, but she finally slipped it in with Lexi's note and the photo.

Trina squeezed her shoulder. "Are we good?"

"We're good. And I think I hear hot chocolate calling my name." They followed a path lit with paper luminaries through a side gate to the backyard.

"I should have brought some wine or maybe stuff for

s'mores? What does one bring to a 'campfire' party?" Scarlett asked.

"I've got us covered." Trina held up a tin labeled Milk Chocolate-covered Birch Caramels as Fisher approached.

"Hey! Glad you made it. Did you have trouble finding the house?" He must have been feeling especially festive because he leaned in for hugs with both, and that was a first with any of her coworkers if she didn't count Trina when she was attempting to distract Scarlett from reading incriminating blog posts. Fisher pointed them to bins filled with hand warmers, wool beanies, and fleece headbands.

Scarlett claimed items from each. "Fisher, hope you don't mind that I tagged along. How is your family going to feel about Scrooge coming to their get-together?"

He laughed. "They might take it as a challenge. You should know, though, my mom has enough Christmas spirit for everyone. In case you couldn't tell." He gestured to the wide expanse of patio and snow-covered lawn where every space was lit up or ornamented. The sweet way he talked about his mother one-eightied the view Scarlett had of him all these months. Seeing someone at home had a way of doing that.

"It's beautiful," Trina said.

Fisher introduced them to his parents, Ross and Winnie Banks, followed in quick succession by several siblings, a grandpa, two aunts, an uncle, and a collection of adorable nieces and nephews, none of whose names Scarlett would remember. Nor their faces either because so little showed through the space between beaver hats and scarves. Hats just like the one Gil wore. But they were welcoming and warm, a feeling that lingered with Scarlett despite what the thermometer said.

After her turn at the hot chocolate bar, she wandered to the edge of the patio close to one of several barrel fires that warmed the area. She felt lighter somehow as she watched the kids running and giggling and building a fort. Their shouts were a joyful noise sounding through the half-light. The scene brought back memories of winter weekend trips to Flagstaff to find snow for tubing and snowball fights.

"Excuse me," said a small, but insistent voice.

Scarlett glanced down to find a rosy-cheeked cherub

peering up at her from a fluffy pink bundle of hat, coat, and gloves.

The girl tugged on Scarlett's parka, for not the first time, according to the tone of her "excuse me." Apparently the gesture hadn't penetrated the layers.

"Will you be an angel with me?" she asked, her brows and nose scrunching up with her question. She held out a sweet, thickly-mittened hand.

An unexpected flash of memory tickled Scarlett's senses. Anthony at the Halloween party: "Can she read the book to us Dr. P?" "Dr. P, is this your new girlfriend?"

She took the girl's hand. "What's your name, sweetheart?"

"E-li-za." She pronounced each syllable.

"You want to make snow angels, Eliza? I'd love to." They dropped onto the ground and flapped their wings in unison, then stood to briefly admire their creations before sidestepping a few paces to do it all over again.

"We're twins," was Eliza's delightful response, and Scarlett had to agree. She felt like she was five again. On about the fourth angel, she began to wonder where Alan and Gil would fit into the scene. Who would be in the snow with the angels, and who would be a permanent fixture next to the fire with a drink in his hand?

Trina pulled her inside to the line for dinner, sparing further reflection. A fire in the fireplace cast a glow throughout the great room. Loosening her wool scarf, Scarlett sat as close to its warmth as she dared, enjoying the food, even the fish pie and smoked salmon, and the good-natured chatter that existed in families. At least families like this one. She was particularly entertained watching Trina watch Fisher tease a nephew and then be ribbed in turn by an older brother. All in good fun.

Before long Winnie gathered them back outside to circle a roaring fire in an area further lit up by spotlights. They began the way Trina had explained by writing on slips of paper and throwing them into the flames. Scarlett wrote hers quickly. She hadn't read Lexi's entire note yet, but it was time to let it all go.

Then Scarlett maneuvered close to Eliza, and the little girl was happy to settle in next to her for the singing led by her Grandpa Banks. They sang about Frosty and Santa while the children's eyes brimmed with anticipation. When Ross asked in mock confusion, "What should we sing next?" the older, experienced grandchildren called out, "Jingle Bells, Grandpa!" By the time the chorus rang out noisily, real jingle bells combined with their voices, and Santa Claus appeared to shrieks of delight.

He passed out gifts for everyone, calling each name from youngest to oldest, creating a flurry of gloves removed and paper ripped open. Even Trina was invited up to receive a gift, and then Santa read Scarlett's name. Her first thought was a confused, *Someone here has my same name?* But with a bit of prodding she accepted Santa's offering and returned to her spot in the circle next to Eliza. The gift was wrapped in gold paper embossed with delicate white angels holding green, candle-lit wreaths, almost too beautiful to tear into.

"You got a Christmas present too," Eliza exclaimed.

Trina nudged her elbow from the other side. "Looks like The Ghost of Christmas Present."

"Did you arrange this?" Scarlett glanced at her friend while removing her gloves.

"I knew nothing about Santa Claus coming, I swear. I only texted Fisher this morning that I was bringing you."

"Open it," Eliza prodded.

The Ghost of Christmas Present? Scarlett slid a finger under the tape to break the seal, then pulled back the wrapping to reveal a box. She opened that, and nestled inside protective packaging rested a snow globe containing an igloo and a reindeer. A Christmas wreath, with a banner across it that said Alaska, hung like a collar around the animal's neck. She shook the globe, and the glittery snow danced.

"Awww, Alaska's your Christmas present, Scarlett." Trina placed an arm around her.

Almost as quickly as he had arrived, Santa Claus delivered the last gift and disappeared into the shadows of the side yard. As if that was their cue, Fisher and his brothers added logs to the fire while his great-grandpa pulled out a harmonica and began an intro to "Silent Night." Soon everyone was adding their voices as the fire crackled and the night chill was kept at bay.

Later, Scarlett returned a sleepy Eliza to her parents, and

CHRISTMAS FUTURE

Trina left with Fisher to help with food cleanup. Scarlett slipped into a seat next to Fisher's Mom, who was on strict instructions not to lift a finger. They gazed at the dwindling fire, enjoying the quiet.

Finally Scarlett spoke. "Thank you so much, Mrs. Banks. Tonight was perfect in every way. And thank you for the gift. It's beautiful." She patted the box cradled in her lap.

"Please call me Winnie." The woman placed a gloved hand on hers. "Don't take this the wrong way, but I hope it lifted your spirits."

"So Fisher told you about me." It was more a statement than a question.

"I'm the one born in New Jersey." She squeezed Scarlett's hand before withdrawing.

Yes he did. But somehow it didn't matter. Not anymore. Not with someone as generous and kind as Winnie Banks.

"Times like these with family are my favorite. What about you? Christmas in Arizona must be different without snow."

"Actually one of my favorite traditions was borrowing snow gear and going up to Flagstaff every year with tubes and sleds. I thought I was cold then. I had no idea. But I loved the fire pit in our backyard, and singing Christmas carols."

"And you still love those memories in spite of what happened last year?"

"You've heard that story too?"

"Fisher likes to talk about his work." She laughed at that. "He means well."

The quiet wrapped around them again as the question about memories played in Scarlett's head.

But the woman wasn't finished. "One Christmas, one event, doesn't have the power to wipe away all the rest, just as one event can't steal away all the goodness in a person. Your heart's still there, you just need to uncover it."

"You mean let it thaw, because that might not be possible here."

"I think it is. Just sit a little closer to the fire."

That's where Trina found her when she was ready to leave. "Look at the sky, Trina. It cleared up. Have you ever seen such brilliant stars? I've witnessed three shooting stars in the time I've been sitting here. This is unbelievable."

"It's Alaska, Scarlett. It's the most amazing place ever. If you'd stick around longer we could even go see the auroras. It's something else."

"The northern lights? Maybe someday." Scarlett leaned in as they walked to the car. "Just wondering, when's the Ghost of Christmas Future showing up?"

CHAPTER 23
Anchorage: 22°
Los Angeles: 73°

Text #1: *Not sure where you're at these days, but if you're still in Alaska, you're invited to Thanksgiving dinner. Scarlett will be there if that makes a difference. And sorry I forced Heath's mom to give me your contact information. Don't hate her. She said you had given her some tips about a rash, so that's why she had your cell number.*

Text #2: *It's going to be a super small group. Me, my mom, my Uncle Frank, and my cousin from Fairbanks. And Scarlett. Her engagement to Alan is over, so she could use the company. I can guarantee the turkey will be dry, but my mom makes the best salmon pot pie. It shouldn't be missed. Let me know. Oh, and me and Scarlett got invited to our coworker's parents' house for dessert so there's that too.*

The clues in the rambling text pointed to Scarlett's friend, Trina. Gil didn't understand why Heath wasn't coming to dinner, but it didn't matter. The message was enough to get him on a plane back to Anchorage. He arrived, wine in hand, at the time and place she'd texted, not at all sure what paired well with pot pie of any kind.

Trina and the smells of Thanksgiving greeted him at the door. "Scarlett's not coming" were the first words out of her mouth.

"Did you tell her I was?"

"No. That was my little secret. But I'm so worried about her. The closer it gets to the holidays, the more she seems to be embracing her Scrooginess. It's like a badge of honor or something. I know she has a lot to do, but I was hoping she would take today off."

"She's working?"

"She went to Charlestown. She was on the phone with the mayor, and then she took off."

"She's driving in this weather?" That didn't seem like something she would do.

"I know. I told her not to."

Gil followed Trina into the small, square kitchen, where he met the group assembled exactly as she had explained in her text. He handed the wine to Trina's mother, but without Scarlett there he somehow felt as if he was crashing someone's else's party.

"Please, don't take this the wrong way, but can I get a rain check on dinner? I don't know, I just think I should go find her."

"Excellent idea, Gil." Trina's eyes brightened with her smile. "Tell her you brought gravy."

"Gravy? What?"

"Yeah," she said, as if it made perfect sense.

Gil gazed at the stove. "But you're not actually going to give me some gravy?"

Trina waved him away. "Just do it. She'll know."

"Okay. If you say so." He didn't prod her for more of an explanation.

"The site is just outside Charlestown. You can't miss it."

"One last thing, Trina. You're positive she's not engaged anymore?"

"Gil, that blankety-Blankenship has sailed."

He shrugged in confusion.

"That's Alan's last name. Blankenship. Never mind, just go." She shooed him out the door.

Soon he braved the snow that was coming at a steep slant across state route 3 north. Traffic was nearly nonexistent. Smart people were home with their turkey and salmon dinners. As impatient as he was, he forced himself to drive carefully, deciding this was no time to get stuck in his first Alaskan snow bank.

Scarlett had driven a hundred miles to Tucson to find him, so it was no big deal that he would drive half that to Charlestown. *But tack on over three thousand miles by air. That was extreme.*

He was no expert in snow conditions either, so the drive took double the time it would have under normal conditions. At least he hadn't come across any stranded travelers, namely an Arizona driver named Scarlett.

Anchorage: 22°
Phoenix: 68°

Scarlett took a seat next to Micki Blanding at A Fresh Tart, where they were the only potential customers. "I'll have the strawberry tartlets and coffee," she called to the woman at the counter before turning to the mayor. "I hope I won't make you late for dinner. I just had an idea that couldn't wait, and I wanted to show you in person. Can we step outside for a minute? I know that's about my limit in the cold these days." She motioned, and Micki followed her out onto the sidewalk.

"Someone told me that this town has wanted a Dickens Village for a long time, but look, you already have one." Scarlett extended her arm. "Mayor, imagine Charlestown's Main Street decked out in Old World lamp posts hung with pine and berry wreaths. Volunteer actors walking the area dressed as characters from "A Christmas Carol," even Scrooge himself. Father Christmas at one end and a grand, candle-lit tree at the other. Electric candles, of course. And that site they're clearing outside of town? It's perfect for extra parking with a shuttle." Scarlett breathed into her cupped hands, her enthusiasm building. "This could work, and at a fraction of the cost."

Micki gazed to the end of the street and back again. "The Dickens Foundation," she stated.

"Excuse me?"

Micki's saucer eyes didn't blink. "About a year and a half ago an English professor at the community college told me about a foundation he was working with from London. He'd received grant money to write a book for them for charity." She seemed to brighten at the memory, and her words spilled out. "He spoke to them about Charlestown and they were very excited, at least I thought so. I remember he mentioned our downtown and someone had even come to take pictures of it. When the professor passed away, though, that seemed to be the end of it. I never heard another word."

Professor Pennington's manuscript. *Did Gil know it was written with grant money and he sold it to a publisher anyway?* She immediately scolded herself. It was not her business. But a Dickens Village was, and the perfect plan had grown out of the Scrooge character himself. He was the center of *A Christmas Carol.* He just needed a London street as a backdrop. "How much do you want to bet that there's unclaimed grant money for this project from the Dickens Foundation?"

Back inside the café, the mayor tapped her fingernails along the tabletop while Scarlett gripped the edge of it. Finally Micki looked up, moisture rimming her eyes. "Let's do it."

Scarlett's relief forced her gaze heavenward toward the white twinkling lights that crisscrossed the rafters like garland, her weeks of work and worry exhaled all in one breath.

"And Dickens carolers, right?" Micki asked.

Scarlett breathed in the aroma of the sweet strawberry tart in anticipation of her first bite. "Oh, yes. Lots and lots of carolers."

Once Micki left her alone, Scarlett downed her coffee and wrapped her last tart in a napkin to take to Trina. She approached the counter. "Thank you so much. I'll go so you can enjoy dinner with your family."

"I'll be closing soon, but come anytime. Happy Thanksgiving to you."

"To you too." Scarlett pulled on her gloves and stepped out onto the sidewalk right into Gil Pennington. "Gil? What are you doing here?"

"Trina was worried. The snow's coming down pretty thick."

"I mean what are you doing in Alaska?"

He looked up at the sign above the door. "Maybe I'm here for a fresh tart?"

She narrowed her eyes at him. Then she remembered the recording session at KWIX. He was in town with Carole.

"Trina gave me a message for you. In my defense, I have no

CHRISTMAS FUTURE

idea what it means. She said to tell you I brought gravy."

Scarlett clapped a gloved hand over her face, attempting to hide her reaction. It was a cross between wanting to laugh, cringe, cry, all at the same time. Between wanting to call Trina and say, *Cheese and crackers, girl, what are you doing to me?*

Instead she did none of the above. Gravy was a hypocrite. Kissing other people when he was still engaged, blaming her when she did the same.

"That was kind of you to drive up here," she said. "If you wouldn't mind letting me follow you back, that would be appreciated." She headed to her car and tried not to think about him trailing her, watching her step gingerly all the way down the snow-covered sidewalk while wondering about her odd reaction to the mention of gravy.

And why do I care so much about what he thinks?

Micki had agreed to her plan, but that meant there was work to do to transform Charlestown's Main Street by the first weekend of December. She needed no distractions. Following Gil's lights and tire tracks on the way to Anchorage, she focused on the work ahead.

When that became overwhelming because the road required too much of her attention, she allowed herself to revel for a quarter of a mile or so over the success with the Christmas spirit promotion. The magical evening spent with Fisher's family had echoed Marie Pennington's mantra of the noise and quiet of the season. It also cemented an idea in her mind first sparked by Trina. Though Scarlett had been dropped off late after the party, she went straight to her computer to finish the graphic with a title for the campaign: *Jingle Bells & Silent Nights.*

The sponsors featured on the card ranged from Arctic Valley's Tube Park to Anchorage Symphony Orchestra; from Santa Claus and Christmas in Ice at the North Pole to Charlestown's Dickens Village. In between the sponsors listed were winter holiday ideas that didn't cost a thing but would pay back in memories.

She emailed it off to the printer, and early Monday morning her inbox filled with praise for her design. Daniel heard about it before she could tell him, and it wasn't long until Fisher, Jared, and even Hannah had stopped by her cubicle to congratulate her.

When they arrived at the city limits, Scarlett honked her horn a couple of times as a thank you, then took the exit toward her apartment. She'd send her regrets to Trina, but still she felt a little awkward about turning off. She and Gil hadn't discussed exactly where they were going once they got back to Anchorage, and she wouldn't have the chance to thank him formally for his help. She could send a brief text when she got home, but that was a cellular road best not traveled anymore.

She pulled into Ruby's, thankful to find it open and offering turkey dinners. "Happy Thanksgiving." A young man, looking smart in a black shirt, black apron, and red tie, greeted her as she approached the register. She pulled out her wallet and something hard and smooth came with it. The rock with Bah! Humbug! in red letters across its face. Planted by Gil.

Back in her car, she brought up Trina's number on her phone. "Hey, Trina. Hope I'm not interrupting dinner."

"Just dishes, but where are you. Why didn't you come back?"

"No, the question is why and how did you send Gil up to Charlestown? And gravy? Really?"

"Scarlett, listen to me. He's your Ghost of Christmas Future."

Scarlett breathed and she could see the puff of air even in the car. "No," was all she could think to say, but her brain had a mind of its own, spinning thoughts she didn't want to speak out loud.

Trina's tone softened. "I was right about the other ones, wasn't I? Lexi and her letter from the past, and enjoying your present which is Alaska."

"Well, the guy certainly is haunting me everywhere I turn. Anyway, I just got home, so I have to go or my food will get cold. I am really sorry about missing dinner, though. Please, tell your mom for me. Work. You know, the usual excuse for a Scrooge."

She hung up and took a moment to reflect on the day. To marvel that Gil Pennington was in Alaska when she had been so sure she would never see him again. She relived the relief she'd felt when her engagement to Alan had ended earlier in the week. *Finally.* After their disastrous Halloween weekend he knew what

CHRISTMAS FUTURE

was coming and had actually preempted her ending it by calling Sunday to breakup. He couldn't help mentioning all the girls he'd meet and hang out with on his family's trip to Hawaii.

With his mother along. Scarlett kept the jab to herself. Instead she was apologetic, explaining that her internship in Alaska had gotten in the way of their relationship.

She hadn't planned on meeting someone like Gil. But was he lost to her? Was it too late for her Scrooge-like heart to change?

As sad as Thanksgiving dinner for one sounded, she was grateful to bundle up on the couch with light music playing and turkey, cranberry stuffing, and pumpkin pie to savor. She stared off into the glow of the space heater, trying to ignore thoughts of Gravy, humbug rocks, and ghosts of past, present, and future. But even that was a form of thinking about them.

She picked up the copy of *Dickens at Christmas* from the side table and started in on chapter one.

CHAPTER 24

Anchorage: 19°
Los Angeles: 73°

At Trina's urging, Gil showed up at KWIX at noon Friday, but he fought the persistent feeling that he was being a stalker. Scarlett made her opinion clear. He came all the way from LA, and she had walked away and driven away. She thanked him for being kind, and then with two short taps of her horn she was gone. The sound had haunted him as he wrestled with hotel bed sheets and a thick down comforter—and sleep eluded him.

He glanced a bit anxiously in the direction of VIP parking on his way into the building. If he wanted to see Scarlett, visiting the KWIX set during the recording session meant seeing Cari as well. They hadn't spoken since their breakup over the phone.

After lingering in the hallway he finally got the attention of one of the assistants. "You can go on in," he told Gil. "You've only missed Carole's first two segments."

Lights blazed on a flurry of activity on set, with various staff straightening Cari's collar, dabbing her face with a makeup brush, and arranging and rearranging ingredients and dishware on a long counter in front of her. Darkness ruled everywhere else, so maybe he would go unnoticed.

Abruptly everyone stepped out of the camera angle, and voices from the main set singsonged from the sound system. "The gift-wrap ideas were absolutely gorgeous, and with a great Alaskan feel to them, so no more excuses, Sam. You'd better do up something nice for your wife this year," a woman's polished TV voice said. Gil hadn't met the News at Noon team.

The guy that must have been Sam answered. "Well, I'm no Christmas Carole, but I may give some of her ideas a try."

CHRISTMAS FUTURE

"That's exactly who we're talking about. Let's check in with Carole and see what she has in the oven this time." The woman again.

"Thank you, Aurora. And, Sam, I'll be happy to help you out with your wrapping issues." Cari broadcast a smile and clasped her hands in front of her. "Today is cookie day because you can never have too many cookies at Christmas, right? But this one has a twist, so, moms and dads, pay attention." She gestured toward a red plate, and the camera went in close for a shot of a dozen or so black, lumpy cookies. "We're going to make Lump of Coal Cookies." She began to explain the ingredients and dump them in a mixer as she chatted. She was a natural in front of the camera.

Gil didn't see Scarlett anywhere. Maybe her segment was over.

Aurora spoke again. "I think I see these in your future, Sam. Carole, will you give him a test taste, so he'll know what to expect on December 25th?"

"Of course."

"Okay, okay," the male host said. "Carole, continue mixing, and we'll check back in a few minutes."

"I have an idea, Sam. We spoke earlier to Scarlett Ambrose about the Christmas spirit project that she's been working on."

Gil had missed her.

Sam turned to the television-viewing audience. "Don't forget to fill out your entry forms to win an Alaskan adventure." He rotated toward Aurora again. "My kids love going to Christmas in Ice in North Pole every year, as I'm sure yours do, but we were let in on a little surprise that's happening on Main Street in Charlestown."

"That's right. And I am so excited for *A Christmas Carol*–themed street. Now we didn't mention this before, but a popular local blogger called Scarlett out, saying she was a Scrooge. I think we should bring her back to taste the Lump of Coal cookies. I'd like to get her take on all this."

"After this break we'll be back with Christmas Carole to see if those cookies are getting black enough, so be checking to see who's on the naughty list at your house." Sam finished and theme music played.

"Did they really just call me back?" A disembodied voice sounded from the shadow. It was Scarlett. She was still here.

Relief washed over him. "Afraid so," Gil replied.

"When they told me to stick around, I probably should have ignored that." She mumbled something else about making the best of it. How she'd worked too hard to back down.

Aurora and Sam returned while Gil watched Scarlett get the same treatment to clothing and makeup that Cari had received. When she was put in place behind the counter, one of the hosts introduced her again and asked how it felt to be called Scrooge.

"Have you read *A Christmas Carol*? Scrooge's message is one of the most beloved at Christmas time. He learns how to keep Christmas well. Thanks to some new friends I've met here in this beautiful state, I'm finally beginning to understand what that means myself." As natural as Cari seemed in the limelight, Scarlett glowed. But it was her words that caught his attention.

"That is beautiful, Scarlett. I don't think she deserves the Lump of Coal cookies at all, Sam."

"I agree, Aurora."

The camera close-upped on Cari, effectively cutting Scarlett out of the shot. Cari finished the segment with the news anchors and a few children as taste testers. Theme music played again, and it was done.

Gil watched them head in his direction. "I really like what you said, Scarlett," his ex said. "Especially since they didn't prepare you for it. You should let them know that is not acceptable."

"Thank you. You're very good at what you do." They were tossing out compliments like the pesky holiday glitter his sister used to craft with.

"I agree with everything that was just said." Gil shrugged and gestured to both of them.

"Gil!" Cari leaned in to give him the briefest of hugs. "That's nice of you to come support me, but you didn't have to do that."

"I . . . uh." He looked at Scarlett. He couldn't read her face.

"Hudson." Cari stopped the producer on his way past. "I thought I was pretty clear about no children during my segments. You know I can't get sick."

CHRISTMAS FUTURE

"Yeah, I heard." He kept on walking. "Nice job, Scarlett," he threw over his shoulder.

"Don't mind him," Cari said. "He's just mad that I'm leaving for the jewelry show."

Gil noticed Scarlett's eyebrows go up, and she opened her mouth as if she wanted to say something, but Cari clutched her arm and spoke first. "You don't know how happy I was when Gil finished that reservation clinic stuff. I mean the kids there with their runny noses and coughs. He'd come back on weekends and I'd be like, 'Don't touch me, sanitize everything.' I don't even know how he could stand it."

He watched Scarlett's eyebrows lift again.

"I'm pretty sure LA kids get runny noses," Scarlett said. "Or maybe not. I don't know actually." She grit her teeth into a grin.

This would be the last time he would ever have to explain it. "For the record, it was not a reservation, though if it was, I would have been fine with that. I loved every bit of my time there."

"You would, Gil." Cari pawed his shoulder.

"Do you mind if I speak to him for a second." Scarlett looked at Cari as if asking her permission.

"No worries. I have to go." Cari leaned toward Gil's ear, her eyes flashing. "Let me know when you're back in town. I want to introduce you to Jonah." She pressed her lips to his cheek before leaving.

Gil held back, wanting to put space between Cari and any dialogue with Scarlett. Apparently Scarlett didn't feel the same, so he followed her exit from the studio toward the north lobby that led to the parking structure.

Without warning she stopped him near a grouping of fake potted trees, a question in her eyes. "I need to ask you one thing that's bothering me."

Something is bothering her? That might not be the best start to the kind of conversation he wanted to have.

"Did you find your dad's manuscript?" she said.

That's her question?

"I did finally. I sent it off to that publisher, and we're just waiting for a contract." His answer didn't do a thing to clear the discomfort in her look.

"I realize it's none of my business." She paused as if reminding herself of that fact. "Really I don't even know why I'm bringing it up." She looked away toward the exit.

"What?"

"I don't know. It just seems like your dad was the kind of person who would honor his commitments. And maybe you were the kind of person who would want to make sure that happened."

Gil put up his hands in defense, but he had no idea what he was defending. "I don't know what you're talking about."

"Your dad's manuscript. You sent it to a publisher when a foundation had contracted him to write it."

"Foundation? What foundation?" The insinuation blindsided him. "You're accusing me of something that I don't know anything about."

"You didn't know a foundation from London gave your father a grant to compile Dickens' letters?"

"Absolutely not." He forced a breath, though it did nothing to lessen the tightening across his chest and jaw line.

"Oh." She looked off over his shoulder again.

He ran his hand across his forehead. "How do you know so much about it?" he asked.

"Apparently before your dad passed away he was helping to obtain a grant for a Dickens Main Street in Charlestown. The mayor told me he had received his own grant to write a book, so he had an in with them. She thought the whole thing had been dropped, and she forgot about it until yesterday. We called them, then they called back this morning and explained the money was still available. They also shared that they had been trying to reach members of your dad's family without success."

Gil dropped back against the wall, his legs straight, but barely holding him up. He opened his mouth and closed it again.

"Gil Pennington? I never expected to see you here." Darlene stepped toward him with a flowered canvas tote swinging at her side. "I thought you were long gone. Back to greener pastures and all that."

"I, uh," he stumbled.

"Well, I have a package for you." She held open the outsized bag to reveal a brown box labeled with "GP" in black

CHRISTMAS FUTURE

marker. "You've saved me postage and a trip to the post office. Funny thing. I was at my sister's in town watching the news and saw your girlfriend Cari on that Christmas show. I thought why not bring the package here to see if she would take it back to California. I hope that was okay even though I'm not sure where you're at these days as far as she's concerned. Oh, and you were on the TV too." She seemed to finally notice Scarlett. "We laughed so hard about those coal cookies. If Stan were alive, I'd be mixing him up a batch just to tease him."

"So the package?" Gil prodded.

"Yes, from your dad's place. It may have gotten moved in the storage room, I'm not sure. But I was going to email you for your address and ship it off to Los Angeles." Darlene looked at Scarlett again. "So you're the girl from the blog. The one with no Christmas spirit."

"That would be me," Scarlett replied, but Gil could tell her smile was forced.

"Oh, well, you look perfectly fine to me." Darlene patted her arm, then busied herself with freeing the package.

Gil caught Scarlett's gaze, but suddenly she slipped something smooth and hard into his palm and mouthed the words *Goodbye, Gil.* Just as quickly, she stepped to the exit to insert a key code. The doors whooshed open and she vanished into VIP parking.

"Here you go." Darlene held the package out to him.

He dropped the Bah! Humbug! rock into his pocket and took the box, hefting the unexpected weight of it for one its size. She helped hold it steady as he pulled out car keys to slice through the tape. Inside, cushioned with tissue paper and packing peanuts, was the nativity. In a small padded envelope, he discovered the tools which his dad had used to so lovingly carve it for his mother.

CHAPTER 25
Anchorage: 17°
Phoenix: 65°

When the elevator doors opened on the Department of Commerce, Community, and Economic Development Monday morning, Scarlett left her hat, scarf, and gloves on a chair and marched straight to the break room. She promptly returned to the lobby with the scotch pine in tow and set to work smoothing out the crippled branches. As she rehung errant light strands, the elevator doors opened again and spilled out a trio.

"Merry Christmas! You're late," Scarlett said. "Hannah, will you grab the boxes of new ornaments from the floor here? Do you have the candy canes I texted you about, Trina?"

Daniel stared. "What are you doing, Scarlett?"

"I'm decorating a tree." She rolled her eyes.

"No, *cheechako*. You're done. The entry forms are being distributed everywhere. The Dickens Village decorators are busy working. I thought you'd be on a plane heading to 90 degrees."

"Don't call me that, Daniel. I've been here for months, and today I'm experiencing a new low of seventeen degrees. Apparently I have to start plugging in my car at night and soon I'll have to eat lunch outside if I ever want to see the sun. So give me a little credit." She couldn't leave. She hadn't done any of the activities she'd highlighted in the Jingle Bells & Silent Nights publicity, and she wouldn't miss the Dickens Main Street tree lighting on Friday for anything.

Trina had continued down the hallway to their cubicle and she motioned to Scarlett. "It's okay if your cousin didn't get the

CHRISTMAS FUTURE

candy canes," Scarlett said when she joined her. "I'm going up to North Pole for Christmas in Ice this week anyway."

"I don't want to talk about candy canes."

Scarlett burst out laughing. "It's December tomorrow. It's finally okay to discuss candy canes. By the way, thank you for teaching me about *A Christmas Carol*."

"You should thank Gil for that. His dad was the expert, and from what you've told me about his parents, he actually lived it. But listen to me. I want to talk about airplanes."

"Didn't you hear what I said to Daniel? I'm not leaving."

"Gil is! He just texted me and said he was heading to the airport."

Scarlett ran her fingers through her loose curls. "So?"

"So he broke off his engagement to Carole."

"No." Scarlett waved away Trina's statement. "I saw them together at the station Friday."

"All I know is I asked and he answered."

"Trina, he has other plans, and they don't include me."

"You've never given him the chance to explain himself. Not since Arizona. Not since my admittedly failed engagement party. Not since Thanksgiving. You broke off things with Alan, now don't let your future go."

My future?

"Gil flew all the way from LA to see you on Thanksgiving day."

"He did? He did! So I should go? You're right. Yeah. I'm going to go." Her mind and feet seemed to be moving in slow motion. "Alaska Air. Right? He flew that before."

Trina grabbed her shoulders and forced eye contact. "Scarlett, not Alaska Air. He said a private company called Northern Lights Alaska. Go! Tell Gil how you feel about him."

She flew out of the office to her car and headed south toward Ted Stevens International Airport, thankful for clear roads gifted by dutiful snowplows. She was going to find Gil, just as she had in Arizona. This time empty-handed, without the excuse of books for kids. She felt the same nervous anticipation about what to say, how to explain herself. This wasn't a hundred miles, though. It was a short five-mile trip that was taking forever.

Somehow she parked and asked directions to Northern Lights, and soon their slogan greeted her: *North to Home*. She didn't even have to pass through security.

On the drive over, she'd imagined herself in a movie, dodging impatient travelers, hurdling luggage and small children, but instead the area was quiet. Only a few people waited in molded plastic chairs with a couple more in line at a counter. And then she spied him looking out at the runway through the floor–to-ceiling glass.

She paused to take a breath when an adorable new walker toddled in front of her and fell on his seat. "Maybe I will have to jump over children," she said, causing the little boy's father to snatch him away and Gil to turn at the sound of her voice.

"Scarlett? What are you doing here?"

"We seem to keep asking each other that question," she said, bracing herself at the sight of him. "So I'll answer it. I don't care if you get on that plane and go be a rock-star, fancy doctor in LA and marry Christmas Carole and have five kids and . . . well, maybe I do, but you're going to go knowing that I love you. That I want you to be my Christmas Future." Emotion caught in her throat. *Cheese and crackers*, she was doing well until that last line.

"So is this where I get on the plane or you think I got on the plane? It pulls away and you think I'm gone, but really I'm standing right here?"

"It probably works better with busses. The guy or girl waiting for the bus, but doesn't get on and it pulls away and he or she is standing there. But, yeah, do that. Don't get on the plane. I mean, if you don't want to. I can't compete with LA—"

"I don't think it's going to work."

"I know, I'm sorry." *Stupid tears.* "I shouldn't have pushed you away. I should have—"

"No, I mean, there's no way they're going to let me stand by the plane while I pretend to get on. If I go through that door, then that's it."

"You should have taken a bus or a train. A boat maybe?"

"I wish I'd thought of that. I should have known you were going to show up." He held up his phone. "Actually I did. Trina texted me."

CHRISTMAS FUTURE

"She would." Heat crept up Scarlett's neck and not from her wool scarf. She heaved a sigh. Too late to stop for something minor, as in total embarrassment. "I think the ability to text has taken the romance out of moments like this."

"I don't know. I enjoy texting. At least I have very fond memories of texting with a beautiful, curly-haired blonde over the last month or so."

Her heart did a hop, skip, jump.

"Maybe I don't want to be a fancy doctor in LA, marry that person you mentioned, and have five kids. But I'm not opposed to the five kids part if my wife and I agree on that sort of thing. Or I'll just do whatever she wants because I love her and want to make her happy. Plus I know she's really great with kids."

And her heart continued another couple of skips.

"How about I abandon all previously discussed transportation options and use my legs to walk right over to tell you that I love you. I don't know how, but I do." They closed the gap with an embrace hindered only by thick outerwear. "I don't want to just keep Christmas, Scarlett. I want to keep it with you."

She pulled back to look him in the face, his really nice face that she hoped never, ever broke. "Are you asking me to marry you?"

"I didn't plan this so . . . no?"

"I'm good with that. For now."

Gil began to hum "Last Christmas" into her ear, the part about giving hearts to someone special.

"I hate that song," she murmured.

"You have no Christmas spirit," he mumbled back.

"So I've been told, but lucky for me I know a guy who knows how to keep Christmas well."

The door opened, and a woman announced the boarding of the flight.

"You wanna fly to Fairbanks? I'm meeting a guy about a mobile clinic that serves the outer areas of Alaska. It's about a dozen degrees colder there than here, though."

"Bring it on. I'm layered." She squeezed him a little tighter through her bulky winter coat and his. "As if you couldn't tell."

❉

"Scarlett, look. I'm no longer an orphan!" Trina twirled on Charlestown's Main Street in a deep green Victorian-style dress, her long hair pulled into a sleek bun. "When I was in the play in high school we used to envy the girls that got this wardrobe. Now I've got a petticoat and even a fake-fur muff. I've always wanted a muff." Her enthusiasm bubbled.

"Can I borrow that? It looks warm." Scarlett drew it up to her nose. "Better yet, can I wear it on my face?"

Gil slapped Fisher on the back. "You're looking dapper, my fine fellow."

"Watch it," Fisher replied.

"I told him if he wants to stroll with me he had to look the part." Trina looped an arm through his very Victorian-looking sleeve as Fisher rolled his eyes.

"Where's your grandpa? Scarlett asked. I can't wait to see him as Father Christmas."

Trina squealed. "You're gonna love him!"

"He said he'd meet by the tree," Fisher said.

"We'd better head that way." Scarlett hugged both Trina and Fisher in turn. "Thanks for volunteering."

She continued down the sidewalk with Gil, gloved hand in his, basking in the glow of the lampposts, heat lamps, and electric candles shining from store windows. A Fresh Tart had a line out the door, and every other business seemed to be bustling as well.

"God Rest Ye Merry Gentlemen" competed with "Joy to the World" and "O, Come All Ye Faithful" in a kind of Dickens Carolers sing-off. Every few steps there seemed to be a new quartet because they had all shown up for opening day.

Scarlett spotted proper ladies and gentlemen and others dressed more like commoners or orphans, and all were in demand for selfies. A little guy dressed as Tiny Tim had a line of people waiting to make donations to charity and for the chance to snap a picture. As they approached, Governor Hunt cut in line for his photo op with a cheeky grin and a big check. Scarlett had finally met him for the first time that morning when he flew up from Juneau for the ribbon cutting.

"Miss Ambrose, come on in here. Let's get a picture together," he prodded.

CHRISTMAS FUTURE

After some nudging by Gil, she joined the governor in front of the local paparazzi. "This is going to put us on the nice list. Mark my words," he said.

She beamed at the photographers. *Just send me my bonus.* But really she was happy and grateful to be part of something so magical. It had nothing to do with money. Maybe a little bit due to the guy with the milk-chocolate eyes snapping pictures of her with her cell phone. Her own little paparazzi section.

"Scarlett!" Micki Blanding called to her from near the glorious donated tree at the top of the street. "It's time."

Gil handed Scarlett her phone. "You go ahead. I want to give to Tiny Tim."

When she saw the amount of his check, she released a breathy "whoa" that couldn't be hidden in the chill of the early evening.

"You know Izzy and I settled things with the foundation. We split the grant money, so I can certainly help Tiny Tim out with a big turkey dinner this Christmas." He winked at her.

"Oh, will you do me a big favor? It involves trudging back to the car in the snow for those two gift bags, though."

"You forget I've traveled much farther than that for you."

"Give me your cold, brittle lips, Dr. Handsome." She leaned in close for a kiss and didn't want to leave. "Stop being so warm. I could just stay right here all night."

"You have a ribbon to cut and a tree to light. And I don't want to miss it."

They parted so she could join the mayor, the governor, and Grandpa Banks as Father Christmas. Trina wasn't kidding about his costume. His crimson-colored robe embellished with exquisite gold reindeer prancing along its borders covered gray-green corduroy trousers. His shaggy white beard and trapper boots and hat completed the look that was a cross between Old World Santa and an Alaskan mountain man. Scarlett greeted him with a wink and a warm handshake so as not to force him to break character in front of the crowd. He tapped a side pocket. "I brought my harmonica just in case."

"I'm always ready for a round of 'Silent Night,'" she replied.

Scarlett chatted with the mayor and the governor until she

saw Gil take up a spot near a bench swarming with orphans. She held her phone out to him again for picture taking.

As the governor gave his speech, she smiled dutifully when he mentioned her name and everyone clapped the muted applause of a glove-wearing crowd. Next up, Mayor Blanding spoke. Without blinking once, probably.

Scarlett's gaze moved from Gil to Trina and Fisher down on the right. Next to them stood Daniel and his wife, then Hannah and Jared. Darlene, the secretary at the college, waved at her from the front of the bookstore. Scarlett didn't know Darlene well but she had told Scarlett when they met that she didn't look like a Scrooge at all. She waved back.

Then she didn't have to take a turn speaking because the governor and the mayor had taken so long that everyone was in danger of freezing if they didn't move their limbs immediately. Four grown adults—Scarlett, the two public officials, and Grandpa Christmas—held onto a goofy, humongous pair of scissors as they prepared to cut a ribbon that draped the end of the street.

"Wait, wait." Governor Hunt stopped the proceedings. "C'mon up, Scrooge." A thin, wiry man, the spitting image of the famed Dickens character, emerged from the crowd. Scarlett almost teared up at the sight of him as the cameras flashed. *This is all because of you.* He joined in the scissor holding, and then the mass of people cheered when Father Christmas and Scrooge pushed a button to light up the tree.

Afterward Scarlett found Glenda and Bo, who had been invited down especially for the event. "I have thank you gifts for you." She handed each a brightly colored bag.

"What's this?" Glenda wondered.

"Just a little something."

"A mug," declared Bo, pulling back tissue to reveal a moose on the front of his.

Glenda did the same. Hers read BEST MAYOR EVER. She reached out a hand to grasp Scarlett's. "That's real sweet." It was high praise coming from her.

As they walked away, Gil whispered in Scarlett's ear, "Better not let Micki Blanding see that."

Scarlett linked her arm in his. "Don't even worry about it. I bought her the very same one. I'm an equal-opportunity gifter."

He pulled something from his pocket. "I grabbed us a couple of entry forms on my way past the used bookstore. Someone really talented designed these."

"I'm surprised I can even look them in the face."

"What activity do you want to do first?" Gil's eyes brightened with his question.

She returned his smile. "It doesn't matter because we're going to do all of them over and over every year for the rest of our lives."

Scarlett and Gil mingled along Main Street until the crowds thinned and he pulled her toward the Christmas tree, where the chill air thrummed with the first harmonica notes of "Silent Night." The snow sparkling under the moonlight crunched and squeaked under their feet as they walked.

"I want to show you something." He shrugged out of the small backpack that Scarlett had wondered about all night. He unzipped it and brought out a carved nativity in tones of golden mahogany. One piece of wood featured Mary, Joseph, and the baby Jesus protected by a stable roof.

"Your mom's nativity." Scarlett's breath came out in puffs.

"That my dad carved," Gil added.

"It's part of both of them. I'm so happy you found it."

"I really wanted you to have it."

"No, Gil. You have to give it to your sister."

"I know, but listen. I want to try my hand at carving one for you. We can pass it down along with the stories to our five children and their children."

"Five children, what?" But then she laughed and leaned in close. He tilted up the end of the carving so she could read the inscription: *Keeping Christmas well—GP & MP.*

"Is this the point in the event where I can quote Dickens? Though I might take some liberties," Gil said.

"Go for it, you son of a professor." She melted into his winter coat embrace and smiled at the noise and the quiet of the evening.

"A merry Christmas, Scarlett! A merrier Christmas than you have had for many a year."

FEBRUARY

All the regulars were gathered around Daniel's sturdy wooden desk: Scarlett, Fisher, Jared, Hannah, even Trina, and whoever else from the office cared to fit. The governor waited on video chat, with Jared holding the phone. Daniel wormed his way in through the bodies. "Scooch together," he called out before taking his own seat in front of his computer. He maneuvered the mouse. "Okay, should be getting something any minute."

"I'll be happy if we just beat Ohio," Hannah said.

"And, no offense, Fisher, but how much do you want to bet New Jersey's made the naughty list again?" Jared pumped a thumbs down with his free hand.

"Guys, think higher. The nice list," Trina reminded.

"It just dropped into my inbox. Scarlett, you're our newest employee, and, of course, this was your project. Maybe you should do the honors."

Scarlett moved around to take the seat Daniel vacated. He bent down to open the email with another click of the mouse, but she kept her eyes down. It had been an agonizing almost two-month wait for the new Christmas spirit naughty and nice lists to be announced by the radio station in D.C. But was she ready to find out where Alaska placed, if at all? It would be a huge leap to go from top ten worst to top ten best considering there were thirty states falling solidly in the middle.

"Where do I start? Naughty or Nice?" She took several deep breaths in quick succession while the office filled with differing opinions. She looked up at the screen, her palm on the mouse. "Nice." She decided. "Surely, we're nice."

She scanned the email. That's where it began so she started at the top. "Number one: Washington, D.C."

The room exploded with "No way" and "It figures" before it got quiet again.

"Number two: Pennsylvania. Number three: Tennessee. Number four: Massachusetts," Scarlett read.

CHRISTMAS FUTURE

"The suspense is killing me," Hannah said.

"Number five: Ohio."

"Ohhh." No one liked that one. Maybe because Micki Blanding's sister lived there.

"Number six: Washington. Number seven: Missouri. Number eight: Texas."

"A newcomer!" Jared exclaimed.

"Take it easy. You've got the governor in your hand." Fisher pointed to Jared's phone.

Scarlett fought to keep her eyes from skipping ahead, but it was impossible. Her heart rate had tripled since number one. "Number nine: Mississippi." She paused.

"Say it, Scarlett." Trina said.

"Number 10: Alaska." A cheer went up and plenty of "We did it" and "I knew it."

"Congratulations, Scarlett," Daniel said, and everyone clapped. He led them down the gray fabric corridors of the cubicle city, past the Christmas tree decorated in pink and red hearts to the break room. Coffee and doughnuts all around marked the achievement.

Scarlett slipped away to call Gil, who had flown to Klukwan in southeast Alaska with a small team of primary care doctors. His very first trip with them. "Number ten!" She squealed into the phone when he answered.

"Congratulations. You deserve it."

"Alaska deserves it. Anyone who's been here knows we have the most spirit."

"We?"

She laughed. "California's still on the naughty list, sorry."

"They'll get over it." he replied.

"Kind of like Loren Medical had to. They lost 'The Compassionate Doctor.'"

It was his turn to laugh. "I gave up Loren. You dropped Van Doren."

"That rhymed. You may be a writer like your father." She giggled into the phone. "Nah, you'd better stick to saving lives."

"How's Lexi doing with the grand Van Doren fiftieth anniversary party anyway?"

"She called again last night to complain about Amelia, but

it's a good thing—it relieves her stress and reminds me that I'm glad I'm not the one dealing with it. Or with Alan's mom who keeps inserting herself into the planning. Lexi gave me some great ideas for the Dalton Retirement Party I'm working on. I really do love being able to share our projects with each other even though we're three thousand miles apart." Reconnecting with her old roommate had been one of the highlights of the Christmas season.

Gil purposely cleared his throat. "You know this is the first time we've been apart since December, so fill in the blank: absence makes the heart grow fonder or wander?"

"Wonder!" she exclaimed. "I wonder when is the love of my life coming home."

"Home. I like the sound of that," he replied. "And some day in the future it will even mean the same house."

"Our future." Scarlett sighed into the phone. "I better get back to work but guess who took a break from chopping wood to find cell phone service? My favorite brother Royce. And get this, his wife got on the phone and said they were living in Fairbanks working graveyard shift at a convenience store because they failed at living off the grid. Royce was just too embarrassed to tell us. They invited us up this weekend."

"We should go so I can thank him properly for bringing his cute Arizona sister all the way to Alaska."

"Don't you have to stop in Fairbanks on your way back? I'll get off work early Friday and we can meet in North Pole at that diner on Santa Claus Lane."

"How about Mistletoe Drive? I was there once with the most amazing girl I've ever laid eyes on, north, south, or in between. I believe she owes me a kiss."

If you enjoyed Christmas Future, please consider leaving reviews on Amazon & your other favorite book sites

Thanks, Readers! ~Valerie

ACKNOWLEDGMENTS

This book fueled by...
my husband's encouragement & my family's patience
the best writing friends, Tamara & Peggy,
& other interested readers
Pandora's Indie Holidays Radio station
Google & chocolate
No sleep & a deadline
Equal parts pure grit and utter insanity
One midnight run to Sonic for a chocolate milkshake
& several Sabbath days of worship and grateful, needed rest from labor

Thanks to...
E.P. Bentley for extraordinary editing
Leilani Jones, Anna Taylor, & Peggy Urry for beta-reading
Jamie Hixon for much-needed feedback
Landi Johnson & Jill Marcotte for insights into Alaska
Mike Giberson for professor-related items
Nate Williams for tech stuff
& Lance Ipson for answers to other random questions

& *thank you*, Charles Dickens,
for gifting the world with Scrooge &
A Christmas Carol in 1843
& every year since then!

ABOUT THE AUTHOR

Valerie Ipson loves reading, writing, genealogy, and Hershey's Extra Creamy Milk Chocolate Toffee & Almond Nuggets (can the name be any longer?). She lives in Mesa, Arizona, and *Christmas Future* is her first published Romance. She is also the author of one YA novel titled *Ideal High*. She hopes she can give readers the same experience she has enjoyed through the years while being curled up with a good book*!*

valerieipson.com
+check out my Book Love journals on Amazon & B&N+

www.ingramcontent.com/pod-product-compliance
Lightning Source LLC
Chambersburg PA
CBHW050635300426
44112CB00012B/1811